Cyril Posthumus

THE ROARING TWENTIES

An Album of Early
Motor Racing

Cyril Posthumus

THE ROARING TWENTIES

An Album of Early Motor Racing

BLANDFORD PRESS
Poole   Dorset

First published in the U.K. 1980

Copyright © 1980
Blandford Press Ltd,
Link House, West Street,
Poole, Dorset BH15 1LL

British Library Cataloguing in Publication Data

Posthumus, Cyril
　The roaring twenties.
　1. Automobile racing – Pictorial works
　I. Title
　796.7'2'09042　　　　GV1029.15

ISBN 0 7137 0967 7

Typeset by Tonbridge Printers
in 11/13pt V.I.P.
Century Schoolbook and
Printed in Great Britain by
BAS Printers Limited, Over
Wallop, Hampshire.

Frontispiece:
L. Densham (Brescia Bugatti)
about to be overtaken by
C. M. Harvey (Alvis) in the 1927
200 Miles Race at Brooklands.

CONTENTS

Foreword vii
Introduction viii

1 **Getting Going Again** — 1920–21 1
2 **Consolidation** — 1922–23 16
3 **Golden Age** — 1924–25 45
4 **Fading Glories** — 1926–27 75
5 **Sports Cars Ascendant** — 1928–29 112

Postscript 143
Index 144

FOREWORD

Like many a youngest child in a family, I was fated to get my toys, comics, bicycle and news second-hand. I first became aware of motor racing as distinct from just 'motors' when one of my brothers came home from a cycle trip to Weybridge. He talked excitedly of a place called Brooklands, as a result of which I began to study the boys' magazines and cigarette cards more closely, and to read Alfred Edgar's racing stories with their exciting illustrations. One day our daily paper bore pictures of a big crashed white car, and my mother, soft-hearted and kind, spoke of a 'poor Parry Thomas' who had somehow been killed, although she can only have known of him as a name, just as we, her children, 'knew' cigarette card heroes such as Dixie Dean, Jack Hobbs, Jack Dempsey or Steve Donoghue.

A year later there was a big motor race in Ulster, bearing the mystery initials 'TT' and won by Kaye Don, a man who actually lived in *our* village, causing a stir in the local paper and greatly exciting my brothers. By the time I had reached my own 'teens and had pedalled myself to Brooklands on one of my brothers' cast-off bicycles, the thirties had arrived, but I retained a special interest and warmth for the twenties decade of motor racing that I had so narrowly missed. One hears and reads much of the heroic age of the pioneers, but the racing immediately following the Great War was equally exciting, and equally important in the over-all history of the sport.

In a spectacular subject like motor racing, pictures tell the story far better than words, and there are over 200 in this book to show how the cars, drivers and circuits of the day looked. These pictures have come from many sources; from private collections, manufacturers' files, magazines and press agencies. A few came from that modern phenomenon, the autojumble, several from a street market in France, while a sizeable batch was acquired from Spain in exchange for Norton motorcycle spares desperately sought by a Spanish enthusiast.

My thanks go in particular to that arch-collector of motor racing photographs, T. A. S. O. Mathieson, for the loan of several of his precious prints; to Dudley Gahagan, historic racing car driver and another arch-collector, for many rare and interesting photos; and to Geoff Goddard, who not only provided numerous pictures from his own large collection, but also undertook the processing and restoration of illustrations for this book, bringing many tired old prints and negatives back to life.

With so wide a variety of sources, and some that simply are not known, one can but pay respectful tribute to the unnamed photographers of 50 to 60 years ago for their skill in recording so graphically the motor racing history being enacted before them.

C.P. 1980

Opposite: Kaye Don setting a new Brooklands Outer Circuit lap record in August 1929 at a speed of 134.24 mph, driving the 4-litre twelve-cylinder Sunbeam 'Tiger'.

INTRODUCTION

The Challenge: Monsieur Edouard Ballot (centre) poses with two of his four-car team of 4.9-litre straight-eight Ballots at the Paris works, before leaving for the first post-war Indianapolis 500 Miles race in 1919. The drivers are Albert Guyot, on left, and Réné Thomas.

When it is realized that motor racing has been going on now for eighty-five years, the 1920–29 decade emerges as one of outstanding importance in the over-all picture. It brought many decisive innovations, such as supercharging and multi-cylinder engines, the new class called sports car racing, and a famous race, the Le Mans 24 Hours. The massed start was introduced, riding mechanics were largely dispensed with, the Grand Prix category became multi-national instead of exclusively French, with six other nations promoting their own Grands Prix, and organizers began paying prize money where previously the honour of victory had alone sufficed.

Beginning in the shadow of World War 1, the twenties decade blossomed into a mini golden age, then slowly tailed off into the gloom of a world economic depression. It produced some magnificent racing, and some that was deplorably dull; some of the greatest drivers of all time made their names, if not their fortunes, during its span, while some unforgettable racing car designs emerged as masterly examples for others to follow.

At first the great thing was, of course, that the war had really finished. 'San fairy Ann'—the British Tommy's version of *Ça ne fait rien* (meaning broadly 'It doesn't matter' or, in modern parlance, 'So what?') — was the philosophy as the twenties opened; war was to be forgotten and peace enjoyed to the full, and the 'Roaring Twenties' became as carefree a decade as politics and economics would allow, with the Kaiser forgotten and Adolf Hitler an unknown noise in a Germany struggling up from defeat.

People so long deprived of pleasure were justly out to 'make hay' and enjoy themselves, and car manufacturers, too, celebrated after years of dull munitions production with some enterprising, exciting designs, as the early post-war motor shows revealed. There was new, basic transport aplenty, but much luxury too, with suave overhead camshaft 'sixes', straight-eights and even V-12s, wartime aviation practice clearly evident in most of them. While money made from munitions helped many of these cars into existence, enthusiasm rather than abundant cash nourished other enterprises.

In Britain W. O. Bentley, designer of the successful Bentley rotary aero-engine, was laying out a new 3-litre four-cylinder ohc sports car on a tight budget; T. G. John, maker of pistons, was working on a smaller 'four', the Alvis, while two famous sprint specialists, Archie Frazer Nash and H. R. Godfrey, had resumed

In sunny Spain: while the rest of Europe slowly recovered from the Great War, neutral Spain was able to continue motor racing in the small car classes. Here is Santiago Soler, winner of the Circuito Bajo-Panadès in 1919, before the start in his 1100 cc David. This Barcelona-built cyclecar was novel for its final drive incorporating expanding pulleys and belts.

En route *to fame: 21-year-old works tester Enzo Ferrari in his first racing event, the Parma-Poggio di Berceto mountain climb on 5 October, 1919. His CMN (Costruzione Meccaniche Nazionale) had a 3-litre four-cylinder side valve engine, and took him to fourth place in his class.*

production of the famous GN cyclecar which first 'racketed' its way into fame up British gradients in 1913. There were dozens of other new makes of car, from starkly utilitarian to blithely sporting, springing up in the new zest for life, recovery and progress that inspired the post-Armistice scene.

When the exhausted combatant countries recovered their national 'breath' and took the first steps towards rehabilitation, the revival of sport came quickly to mind. Games such as football, cricket, tennis, athletics or cycle racing could restart without difficulty, but a more costly, complex and organized sport like motor racing took longer to revive. Tyres and fuel, let alone cars, were prior essentials, and all were in short supply. So post-war motor racing in Europe began with sprints and hillclimbs, the cheapest and easiest kind of event to promote when facilities were limited.

Neutral Switzerland managed a speed hillclimb at Burtigny, near Geneva, by 1 June 1919, won by Meynet with a pre-war Hispano-Suiza. Britain's first events happened later that same month, with a sprint at Hand Post, Middlesex, won by a

Vauxhall, and a hillclimb at South Harting, Sussex, won by a GN. Denmark, of all places, staged a 'speed records' meeting on the sandy beach of Fanoe Island, off Copenhagen, Fiat of Italy taking the trouble and expense of sending Minoia with a 1914 Grand Prix type S57, the pair winning at an impressive 94.44 mph.

America was even quicker off the mark. Geographically over 3000 miles away, and involved in the fighting only from June 1917, the USA was far less affected by the war and was quickly back in the peacetime groove. Racing took place at Santa Monica, California, as early as March 1919, and meetings at the Ascot asphalt speedway and Uniontown board track quickly followed during that happy spring. Nevertheless, the big revival internationally was the classic Indianapolis 500 Miles race on the famous brick-paved 2½-mile oblong speedway with its four banked corners. 'The bricks', as one observer put it, 'had only been cold since 1916', and on 30 May 1919 the spectacular '500' came back to life, subtitled 'the Victory Stakes'.

The race brought several surprises, the biggest being the participation of a full team of brand new French cars at a time

Great names: American movie star Douglas Fairbanks poses with American motor racing star Ralph de Palma at the 1919 Santa Monica race meeting in California. The car is de Palma's famous 9.9-litre twelve-cylinder Packard with which, earlier that year, he set a new one-way world speed record at 149.875 mph on Daytona beach.

when France, grievously stricken by the war and the loss of over a million of her sons, was still notably convalescent. Leading French car makers busy replanning their factories for peacetime production had agreed not to race in 1919, but one man of influence, Edouard Ballot, upset this truce. He made proprietary engines, not cars, besides turning out countless generator units, pumping plants etc. during the war, and shortly after the Armistice he was persuaded to construct four new and very sophisticated 4.9-litre racing cars to contest Indianapolis in 1919.

That race meant more than mere prestige; there were big money prizes too, the winner taking $20,000 (£4000), while an extra 1919 incentive was 'lap money' of $80 per round for the race leader. With but 120 days, including Sundays and the Christmas holidays, the Ballot design was finalized and the cars built at their Paris works in Malakoff — a remarkable feat in such difficult times aided by much sub-contracting. Ernest Henry, pre-war Peugeot racing car designer, drew up the daring engine specification, with its eight cylinders in line (used for the first time ever), twin overhead camshafts, four valves per cylinder and crankshaft with five roller bearings.

By dint of much scrambling the cars were completed and shipped to the States to challenge the American speedway specialists on their home ground. Their drivers were all French professionals — Réné Thomas, the 1914 winner, Bablot, Wagner and Guyot—and on arrival they found, to their surprise, a rival team of straight-eights built by the American Duesenberg company. Practice showed these to be slower than the Ballots, even though the latter had unsuitable drive ratios and had to fit US-built wheels and tyres. These proved unequal to the pace, and two Ballots departed the race with collapsed wheels, the other two soldiering on between stops to fourth and tenth places. Ironically the race was won by a 1914 four-cylinder Grand Prix type Peugeot — an earlier Henry design — in the hands of the American 'Howdy' Wilcox at 87.12 mph, compared with the unlucky Ballot's record lap at 105 mph.

Gradually the sport resumed elsewhere. Latin enthusiasm brought racing back to Italy by October, with two mountain climbs at Parma Poggio di Berceto and Consuma, both won by a new man, Antonio Ascari, in a 1914 Grand Prix type Fiat. A month later the wealthy and enthusiastic Cav. Vincenzo Florio contrived to hold the first post-war Targa Florio, over four laps of the notorious 67-mile mountain circuit in Sicily. Competitors had something of everything in this race, a fierce gale preceding rain, hail, sleet and snow, followed amazingly by sunshine.

Italy's new hope, Antonio Ascari, skidded in his Fiat, plunged 30 feet down a ravine, and was not found until halfway through the race; future body stylist Giacinto Ghia wiped his Diatto against a rockface, a Peugeot hit a wall, a British Eric Campbell

broke its steering, while Réné Thomas in the one 4.9-litre Ballot competing made his bid for the lead, only to smash an axle against a kilometre stone. Poignantly for France, the victor was another Frenchman in another French car — André Boillot, younger brother of the great Georges Boillot, the pre-war racing ace who lost his life in an aerial dogfight over the Western Front in 1916.

Young Boillot drove a 2½-litre Peugeot built for a 1914 voiturette race which never happened because of the war. After a phenomenally determined drive, during which he left the road six times, he reached the finish, braked hard to avoid excited spectators, and spun, crossing the line backwards. Edouard Ballot, who had come to see his own car win, very sportingly urged Boillot to go back and recross the line the proper way. Boillot did so, then collapsed over the wheel murmuring, we are told, 'C'est pour la France'.

* * *

The big one: America's greatest motor race, the Indianapolis 500 Miles, was resumed in 1919 after a two-year war break. This scene at the first corner of the first lap shows de Palma's white Packard disputing the lead with 'Howdy' Wilcox's Peugeot No. 3 and Réné Thomas's Ballot, with Guyot's Ballot No. 32 in train. Wilcox won the race, while Guyot's was the highest-placed Ballot, in fourth position.

1
GETTING GOING AGAIN
1920-21

With both Indianapolis and the Targa Florio of 1919 won by Peugeot cars, proud France was certainly in the ascendancy as the 'Roaring Twenties' were ushered in. They came in with enthusiasm allayed by doubts. Economically the world did not seem much more sensible than during the war, with a boom in new cars and motorcycles, offset by difficulties in building them, aggravated by shortages of skilled labour and of materials and parts, and by strikes. There was relief in sport, and while the French demanded their Grand Prix back in vain ('America has its Indianapolis, Britain and Belgium their motor shows, Italy her Targa Florio — only la France, it seems, is still deprived of all grand manifestations', wrote Charles Faroux bitterly) Italy talked of running one of their own.

The British, more practically, asked 'What about Brooklands?' After four war years, this famous banked track near Weybridge in Surrey stood unkempt but still apparently usable. Why, then, could racing not be revived there? In truth it had suffered grievously in 1914–18, when the RFC took it over. The constant passage of solid-tyred lorries over its lower stretches, formed of 6 to 8 inches of concrete laid on a mere sand base, caused large areas to break up. Frost and neglect did their fell work too, and bumps and holes were legion, precluding high speed work until extensive repairs were carried out. Persuading the responsible authorities to do this took time, as ever, and Mr Hugh Locke King, the owner, was unable to permit racing at Brooklands again until 1920.

Easter Monday was the big date, but the long-awaited day brought anti-climax. Teeming rain fell, and after running two match races, one between Malcolm Campbell (1912 Grand Prix Lorraine-Dietrich) and J. Moorhouse (Matchless motor-cycle) and the other between Campbell (Talbot) and G. Bedford (Hillman), both won by Campbell, the meeting was postponed to the following Saturday. A smaller crowd attended the 're-run', watching two car races, each split into two heats and a final. The entry list was sprinkled liberally with service titles such as Lieutenant-Colonel, Major and Captain, as was the way then, even though most of the officers concerned had reverted to civilian status.

Nose to tail (opposite): an exciting moment in the historic 1921 French Grand Prix at Le Mans, with the Irish-American Jimmy Murphy in the winning Duesenberg about to pass second man Ralph de Palma, driving a French Ballot. Both cars had 3-litre straight-eight engines and four-wheel brakes, those on the American Duesenberg being hydraulically operated.

Malcolm Campbell's impressive 1912 Grand Prix-type 15-litre Lorraine-Dietrich, seen in road trim with mudguards and lamps (and open exhaust!), as driven from London to Brooklands and other speed venues in Britain just after the Great War. One of his early 'Bluebirds', it won him the first post-war race at Brooklands.

Archie Frazer Nash aviates in 'Kim', his famous 1100 cc twin-cylinder GN cyclecar, when breaking the Brooklands Test Hill record in November 1920. He climbed the 112-yard gradient in 9.37 seconds, and improved his own record five times between 1920 and 1926.

Again it was a Campbell benefit, the ex-Captain winning the first post-war Brooklands race with his big 1912 Grand Prix Lorraine-Dietrich called 'Bluebird'; he also won the final of the second race with his smaller Talbot, while other firsts fell to Mathis and Waverley cars. The role of Brooklands in British racing then was a mixed one. BARC and other club meetings featuring several short races provided good sport in a pleasant garden party atmosphere; handicapping was necessary to even the chances for cars of all kinds, and thus results lacked the impact of those in scratch races. More important to the industry were the testing facilities offered at the track, for cars of all kinds from tourers to single-seater racers could be driven long distances at sustained high speeds, providing invaluable trials of stamina. Record-breaking was another important activity, attracting many specialists in all capacity classes, even the French coming over to use the track pending construction of their own *piste de vitesse* at Montlhéry in 1924.

Apart from Brooklands, British motor racing centred on speed trials and hillclimbs, where the situation was more uncertain. Such events could legally be staged on promenades, beaches or on private land, but the law forbade the closing of public roads for speed events. Broadminded authorities turned a blind eye, however, and providing the public were not inconvenienced and spectators submitted to control such meetings were permitted, and even encouraged for the extra trade they brought to a locality. In the flush of early post-war enthusiasm dozens of events took place at venues up and down the country, renowned performers including Raymond Mays, Archie Frazer Nash, Humphrey Cook, E. R. Hall, George Bedford and many others.

With plenty of Alpine gradients, Italy was well off for hill-climbs, while she also managed a road race revival in 1920 at Mugello, near Florence, on a course almost as hectic as that of the Targa Florio, including a crossing of the Futa pass. It was won by a big burly Milanese with a penchant for opera-singing, Giuseppe Campari, his mount an equally burly 6.1-litre car bearing a new and unfamiliar name, Alfa Romeo. This was an amalgam between the pre-war ALFA and its new proprietor, Ing. Nicola Romeo, who like Ernest Ballot of Paris had produced portable air compressors in quantity during the war, as well as many other useful things. Much, much more would be heard of Alfa Romeo, and also of another of its drivers, Enzo Ferrari, who took up employment with the concern in 1920.

Practice drama: this 3-litre straight-eight Ballot driven by Réné Thomas burst a tyre during training for the 1920 Indianapolis 500 Miles and collided with a Frontenac at over 90 mph. Despite the damage, the car was running 48 hours later, and finished second in the race.

SO NEAR—AND YET SO FAR

At Indianapolis, poor Ballot's hopes for a 500 miles victory were again dashed. The capacity limit was lowered that year from 300 cu.in. (4.9 litres) to 183 cu.in. (3 litres), and a new set of smaller, lighter, prettier Ballots with sleek tails were built. Their 65×112 mm, 2960cc straight-eight engines could turn at 3800 rpm, giving 107 bhp, and again they showed themselves fastest on 'the bricks'. Despite tyre trouble, Ralph de Palma in one Ballot had the lead with 100 miles to go, the other two cars lying third and fourth, and closing on an interloping Monroe. M. Ballot, present at the race, reputedly had just written a telegram for despatch to

Race disappointment: although the Ballots from France lay first, third and fourth 50 miles from the finish of the 1920 Indianapolis race, Ralph de Palma in his white-painted No. 2 suffered magneto trouble when holding a 2-lap lead. He eventually finished fifth, with the other Ballots second and seventh.

A hard day's work: wallowing through seas of mud produced by a week of heavy rain, Meregalli struggles on in his Nazzaro to win the 1920 Targa Florio at the modest average of 31.7 mph after driving for almost 8½ hours.

Paris reading 'Ballot 1-2-3', when the Ballot 'luck' set in; one of de Palm's twin magnetos failed, putting his engine on to four cylinders and dropping him to fifth place. The Monroe moved ahead, whereupon Chassagne was speeded up, only to spin at one of Indy's four turns, damaging his steering and falling back behind de Palma. Réné Thomas, now second, forced the pace but was too late to prevent an American victory.

After Indianapolis came the 250-mile Elgin road race near Chicago, over a rough and tricky 8½-mile circuit whereon de Palma with a single Ballot again met his Indianapolis adversaries. A road course needed good brakes, and his Ballot had these only on the rear wheels. Back in Paris, M. Ballot despatched one of his mechanics, Jean Marcenac, to the States to fit a set of servo-operated front brakes. Thus equipped, de Palma 'walked' the Elgin race with a 67-second cushion over two straight-eight 3-litre Duesenbergs, also with four-wheel brakes but less horsepower. Thus the Henry-designed Ballot had won a race, although the French still had not seen it in a home Grand Prix.

Nevertheless 1920 did bring road racing back to France, albeit in the light car class only. With considerable Gallic pomp the race, the Grand Prix des Voiturettes, was announced for 29 August 1920, at Le Mans. The road course, on the site of a wartime American Army camp, was badly war-torn, loose and neglected, giving the little cars and their occupants a very rough and dusty ride. The war, however, had also given France a distinguished new national defender in the Bugatti car. This product of an Italian artist/engineer, Ettore Bugatti, was built at Molsheim, in Alsace-Lorraine, which before 1914 was under German control, but after the Armistice reverted to France.

The 'German' Bugatti thus became French, and three neat little 1914 1.4-litre 16-valve Type 13s, which had been dismantled, carefully greased and buried at the outbreak of war, were reassembled and very professionally prepared.

They upheld their new nation's honour nobly by occupying the first three places for most of the 256½ miles. Friedrich went on to win, but Baccoli's car suffered plug trouble and dropped to fifth, while the third car, de Viscaya's, broke a connecting rod just three laps from the finish. In those days such failures were concealed whenever possible lest the buying public be deterred, so on learning the truth the crafty Bugatti deliberately unscrewed the car's radiator cap instead of the mechanic doing so, thereby incurring its disqualification on technical grounds and saving the marque's 'face'.

Pit work, 1920: after leading the 1920 Grand Prix des Voiturettes at Le Mans at half-distance, Baccoli's 1.4-litre 16-valve Bugatti developed plug trouble, and then declined to start through a flooding carburettor. In this revealing shot mechanics work on the car, watched by 'Le Patron' Ettore Bugatti himself, on the right. Note the unkempt state of the pit 'road' and the rough, sandy surface; this was the first race held in France after the war.

The success of that race helped the Automobile Club de France (ACF) to make up their minds—their Grand Prix would be revived in 1921, and would be staged on the same Le Mans circuit. It would be open for racing cars of up to 3 litres, and in deference to current manufacturing and tyre problems would be over 325 miles only instead of the customary 500. The winner's prize would be an ACF medal, and entries would cost 15,000 francs (about £600) per car, and had to be in six months before the race; verily racing was different sixty years ago!

French nominations were four Ballots, a Mathis and two Talbot-Darracqs, the latter from the recently-formed Anglo-French Sunbeam-Talbot-Darracq (STD) group. Britain entered two 'Talbots' identical to the Talbot-Darracqs, and Fiat entered three cars, only to withdraw them again, unready and unwilling to race. The list was looking uncomfortably lean when out of the blue came a late entry at extra fees of four Duesenbergs from the USA. Every competing car, bar the rather futile Mathis and one Ballot, was a straight-eight, and every car had four-wheel brakes.

Motor racing in Britain gathered impetus after the war through many hillclimb and sprint meetings. This evocative scene features Felix Scriven's Austin Twenty (a tuned road car stripped of equipment) storming up Beacon Hill, near Loughborough, in 1920, when it made second fastest climb of the day.

'Aviation Hill' or 'The Hump', as they called a crest on the undulating Highland Avenue section of the 8½-mile Elgin (Illinois) road circuit, where cars leapt for 30 feet through the air. This picture of Eddie O'Donnell's straight-eight 3-litre Duesenberg taken during the 1920 race shows the front wheel brakes with mechanical operation, which could not match those on de Palma's winning Ballot. The following year, with hydraulic operation, Duesenberg turned the tables in the French Grand Prix.

7

Rocky road: Guyot's Duesenberg leaping and bouncing off the atrocious top surface of the Le Mans circuit approaching Arnage Corner during the 1921 French Grand Prix.

Race day, incredibly, was a Monday, suggesting how indifferent the august ACF were to public attendance. Alas for Ballot, the favourites, they were roundly beaten by Duesenberg, and the partisan French, still with bitter memories of three white (German) Mercedes finishing 1-2-3 in their 1914 Grand Prix, now had to endure the spectacle of three white and blue cars from the USA finishing 1-4-6, with Ballots sandwiched between the leaders, second and third.

The secret was not only the Duesenbergs' excellent engine torque, but their highly effective hydraulically-operated four-wheel brakes, developed after their defeat at Elgin by Ballot the

All boys together: Count Louis Zborowski's equipe at Brooklands, sporting loud American checker caps—a happy Easter 1921 picture featuring, left to right, Wigglesworth, Miles, Zborowski and the Cooper brothers Jack and R. F. ('Shuggar'), plus 'Chitty Chitty Bang Bang 1'. The tube Wigglesworth is holding was fitted over the starting handle (minus its hand-grip) to swing Chitty's 23-litre Maybach aero-engine into action.

8

previous year. The race was notable for the appalling road surfaces, which broke up under the pace, stones being hurled back at pursuing cars. These smashed the radiators of a Duesenberg and a Talbot, shattering bumps smashed the tank mounts of one Ballot while leading, and one rock shot through the wire screen of a Talbot, severed the cord binding the steering wheel, rebounded and knocked the riding mechanic unconscious. The winning driver, Jimmy Murphy of California, drove with his ribs in plaster after a practice accident, and finished with a holed and empty radiator and two punctured tyres.

The French took their defeat very badly. Although the Americans had been their noble allies in war three years earlier, booing and hissing were mixed with the few cheers when Murphy crossed the line. No national anthem was played, and at the post-race reception the Duesenberg team were received so coldly that they walked out. The ACF took over three months to send the winner's medal — and then misspelt the name 'Duesenburg'. Yet Murphy's average was a prodigious 78.1 mph, plus fastest lap at 83.4 mph on a circuit subsequently used for the Le Mans 24 Hours endurance race, his speeds not being equalled until 1929 despite much improved roads.

VICTORY FOR BALLOT AND BUGATTI

Six weeks later a new Grand Prix, that of Italy, was held on an even faster 10½-mile circuit at Montichiari, outside Brescia. The disillusioned Americans, alas, did not stay for it but went straight home, and Ballot scored their one and only European Grand Prix victory, drivers Jules Goux and Jean Chassagne placing first and second after a non-stop run. The sole remaining finisher was Louis Wagner with a straight-eight 3-litre Fiat, while two others retired, one after leading comfortably and lapping at 96.31 mph. The Italians were as disappointed by Fiat's defeat at Brescia as were the French by Ballot's at Le Mans, but they accorded the victors a much more sporting ovation.

Making history: Jimmy Murphy's white and blue 3-litre eight-cylinder Duesenberg bulleting down the long straight past the pits at Le Mans, when winning the 1921 French Grand Prix—the first and so far only American victory in this classic road race.

A Ballot in the rough at White House during the epic French Grand Prix of 1921. Driver is the French veteran Louis Wagner, who finished seventh after a run dogged by trouble.

Right: Ballot's day came at last in the first Italian Grand Prix, held in September 1921 on the very fast 10.8-mile Montichiari circuit outside Brescia. Here Edouard Ballot doffs his hat to the crowd, with Jules Goux's winning car behind him.

Centre, right: Five 1½-litre 16-valve Type 22 Bugattis lined up outside the works at Molsheim, before leaving for Brescia, Italy, where they took the first four places in the Voiturette race, thereby acquiring the type name 'Brescia'.

Bottom, left: Italy's new star, Pietro Bordino, made fastest lap in the Italian GP at 96.3 mph in this 3-litre straight-eight Fiat.

Below, right: Bugatti wound up a successful 1921 season with first and second places in the Penya Rhin GP at Villafranca, Spain. Here is Pierre de Vizcaya, the winner.

A voiturette race on the same course brought a further French victory, four 16-valve Bugattis careering round with impressive pace and reliability to scoop the first four places ahead of three Brescia-built OMs. Bugattis went on to take the first two places in a new Spanish road race, the Penya Rhin Grand Prix held at Villafranca, and the full 1½-litre Type 22 with 69×100 mm four-cylinder engine became known as the 'Brescia' in honour of its Italian triumph.

That same season, however, brought another and still more formidable voiturette contender in the Talbot-Darracq. Never one to waste design potential, STD's racing chief Louis Coatalen decided to adapt one half of the unsuccessful 1921 3-litre straight-eight Grand Prix Talbot engine, producing a 1½-litre twin-cam 16-valve 'four' which, in unit with a 4-speed gearbox in a compact and tenacious little chassis and light alloy bodywork, proved a remarkable long-term winner. First time out, at Le Mans in the 1921 Grand Prix des Voiturettes, it took the first three places, somewhat demoralizing the British 'opposition', comprising single examples of Aston Martin, Hillman, Alvis and Horstman cars, and beginning a run of voiturettes successes unbroken for six years, totally justifying the sobriquet 'Invincible'.

Establishing a precedent: the triumphant 1½-litre Talbot-Darracq team after scoring the first of many 1-2-3 victories in their very first race, the Grand Prix des Voiturettes at Le Mans in September 1921. The drivers, left to right, are H. O. D. Segrave, who finished third, Réné Thomas the winner, and Kenelm Lee Guinness, second home. Five weeks later these superb little cars placed first, second and third in the 200 Miles race at Brooklands.

Above: Malcolm Campbell, future 'speed king', making fastest time at the Essex County and Southend Automobile Club's Thundersley Church hillclimb in 1921 with his 1912 7.6-litre Grand Prix Peugeot.

Another 'monopolist' also made its début at that Le Mans gathering — the 1100 cc four-cylinder twin ohc Salmson, which carried off the Cyclecar Grand Prix from several French 'home mades' in sweeping professional style, heralding a four-year domination of the 1.1-litre racing class. The year 1921, however, brought yet more of import to motor racing history. To celebrate the centenary of the death of that notorious Corsican, Napoleon Bonaparte, the French-governed island of Corsica in the Mediterranean decided to stage a special race. The course chosen, measuring 68.75 miles per lap from Ajaccio to Bastia and back, was highly spectacular, but significance lay in the race regulations, and in the prize money and other inducements offered to competitors.

Four-seater touring-type cars of up to 3 litres, with compulsory mudguards and windscreens and a minimum wheelbase, were stipulated, marking the birth of the competition sporting car class that was to become famous at Le Mans, and would later in the twenties oust the Grand Prix car from favour. Chenard-Walcker used bodywork with canvas sides to save weight, while two Bignan-Sport cars were specially designed and built, having 3-litre four-cylinder single ohc engines with 16 valves and dry sump lubrication, in very low chassis with big four-wheel brakes, light alloy bodies and special gear ratios.

Right: André Lombard in the first 1100 cc four-cylinder twin overhead camshaft engined Salmson, with chassis descended from that of the British GN, after winning the Grand Prix des Cyclecars at Le Mans in 1921.

Recalling naval camouflage practice in the Great War, H. Kensington Moir's 3.9-litre six-cylinder Straker-Squire appeared at Brooklands with this unique dazzle-painted finish during 1921. Moir is seen winning the Albert Brown Challenge Trophy race at the July MCC meeting.

Breakaway (left): the one and only Corsican Grand Prix, held in 1921, ushered in a new class of racing, the organizers stipulating modified four-seater tourers of up to 3 litres instead of out-and-out racing machines, thus giving birth to sports car racing. Crossing a narrow bridge over a mountain stream is du Berry in a Turcat-Méry. Three major French teams took part.

The organizers offered free transportation of cars from Marseilles and back, and a first prize of 100,000 francs (about £4000). This fell to the veteran driver Albert Guyot in one of the Bignans, with fellow veteran Rougier and Repusseau second and third in Turcat-Méry cars. There were six finishers, the Bignan-Sport driver Delaunay being killed. The race included the scaling of a mountain on each lap, and major troubles included punctures from nails shed by mules, and thick, choking dust, winner Guyot and his mechanic wearing gauze masks over their heads. 'The hardest race I ever ran', he said afterwards.

That one-and-only Corsican Grand Prix set a precedent in race regulations which others soon followed. First to do so were the promoters of the Boulogne Week inaugurated the same year, the programme including a speed hillclimb, sprints, a *concours d'élégance,* and two road races over a rough, heavily cambered 23-mile circuit around the port. One, the Boulogne Grand Prix, was for 1½-litre racing cars; the other, the Georges Boillot Cup, for modified touring four-seaters as in Corsica, the 1921 victor being A. Dubonnet in an Hispano-Suiza.

Les Vainqueurs (above): wearing fine gauze head masks to keep out the choking dust, Albert Guyot and his mechanic win the Corsican Grand Prix in their 3-litre Bignan-Sport. This low-chassis four-wheel-braked forerunner of the sports car was designed by M. Causan. It had a four-cylinder, 8-plug, 16-valve overhead camshaft engine with dry sump lubrication and dual coil ignition, and gave 95 bhp @ 3400 rpm. Bodywork was largely of aluminium and weight was 15.6 cwt. Guyot won the 275-mile race by 35 minutes, but the second Bignan retired.

Novelties abound in this ingenious French cyclecar, the Elfe, seen competing in the 1921 La Turbie hillclimb in the hands of its designer, M. Eugène Mauve. With low tandem seating of driver and mechanic, and an 1100 cc vee-twin engine at the rear, a very low centre of gravity was achieved; steering was by wire and bobbin.

A GERMAN RACE

In early post-war Germany race organizers had to be less discerning, the promotion of a race meeting there in those hard times being little short of a miracle. The opening of a fast new dual motor road in the Grunewald district outside Berlin provided the nucleus of the Avus circuit, which on its 1921 inauguration measured 12.43 miles round. A very mixed collection of cars contested the first *Avusrennen*, the over-all winner at 79.8 mph being Fritz von Opel in a 2.2-litre Opel, with a Benz winning the 1½-litre class.

Beauty at the wheel: the Baronessa Maria Antonietta d'Avanzo, one of Italy's first lady racing drivers, who won the Coppa delle Dame at the 1921 Brescia meeting, driving a 20–30 Alfa Romeo; she raced from 1919 to 1939.

For Britain the season climaxed in October with the 200 Miles Race, the first long-distance event ever staged at Brooklands since its opening in 1907. Organized by the ambitious Junior Car Club, it was limited to 1½-litre and 1100 cc racing cars, each covering 88 laps of the Outer Circuit. A very satisfying entry of thirty-eight cars for the two classes was attracted, including an official Talbot-Darracq three-car team which repeated its Le Mans 1-2-3 act very effectively. First home at 88.82 mph, ex-Major H. O. D. Segrave won the André Gold Cup, while the 1100 cc class proved a tense duel between ex-Capt. A. Frazer Nash (twin cylinder GN) who won, with Frenchman A. Lombard (Salmson) second after crashing into the pits.

In staggering contrast, while the very interesting 200 Miles race drew a paying attendance of 6630 people, the dull Avus affair attracted an estimated 300,000 Berliners — a remarkable pointer to the relative interest in motor racing in England and abroad.

An Opel occasion: Germany's first major post-war race meeting, the 1921 Avusrennen at Berlin's Grunewald track, saw outright and class successes for Opel cars. Fritz von Opel, seen on the left in the helmet, won the main race with a 2.2-litre car at 79.8 mph, watched by some 300,000 spectators, while brother Heinz in the 1400 cc car, seen here, won his category.

The mountain roads between Salo, Zette and Tormini close to Italy's Lake Garda formed a unique 7.6-mile circuit which produced some hectic racing in the 1920s. Here is Deo Chiribiri, third home in the 1½-litre class of the first race, held in 1921, driving an ohv Chiribiri—the marque founded by his father Antonio.

2 CONSOLIDATION
1922-23

Rain was a feature of most 1922 motor races, not least the Isle of Man TT, held over the very difficult 37¾-mile motorcycle circuit. This start picture shows the three marques which contested the TT for 3-litre cars, the cream-painted, flat-radiatored Bentleys on the left, the red Vauxhalls in the centre, and the grey Sunbeams on the right. Sunbeam No. 4 was driven by Segrave: behind is Chassagne's No. 7, which went on to win.

By 1922 motor racing had 'gelled' into a broadly set pattern. At the top was the Grand Prix, which after much grumbling the French had seen revived, only to have it carried off smartly by *les Yankees.* Parallel with it, if slightly less exalted, came USA's Indianapolis 500 Miles, hampered internationally by distance and its special speedway character, and Italy's new-born *Gran Premio.* These were the *grandes épreuves,* and between 1922 and 1925 such events in Europe were run to a new International Formula stipulating a top capacity limit of 2 litres (2000 cc), and a minimum weight of 650 kg (1433 lb). These rules were drawn up by the Paris-based governing body, the Association International des Automobile Clubs Reconnus (or AIACR, the 'FIA' of pre-World War 2 days), and the Americans agreed to adopt the 2-litre Formula for Indianapolis from 1923.

Subsidiary to these races, and within the promotional limits of less than national clubs, came the voiturette racing class for up to 1½ litres (1500 cc), and the Cyclecar or 1100 cc sub-category, while rivalling them was the new four-seater 'touring' class for the nascent sports car. Swelling the calendar still further were more and more hillclimb and speed trial meetings, especially in England where the antiquated laws forbade racing on public roads, and circuit events were thus confined to Brooklands, or to smooth sand beaches such as Southport and Saltburn.

With peace now the *status quo,* and the boom-slump cycle steadying down to more stable production, races further multiplied. In Britain a 500 Miles Grand Prix for the new 2-litre racing cars was mooted for Brooklands in 1922. After much discussion as to whether track or artificial road conditions should be employed, there came the anti-climax of too few entries and cancellation.

Below: the new 'modified touring' class of racing inaugurated in Corsica soon spread to France, Belgium and elsewhere. In 1922 the Belgian Grand Prix was staged over the then new Spa-Francorchamps circuit in the Ardennes, and here the victor, Baron de Tornaco, takes his Belgo-Spanish 3-litre Imperia-Abadal through the turn past the start.

Enter Bentley (below, right): running in their first long-distance road race, the new four-cylinder 3-litre Bentleys did well to finish second, fourth and fifth in the 1922 Isle of Man TT, winning the team award. Here the damp crowd at Craig-ny-Baa watch W. D. Hawkes, fifth man home, sweep into the corner.

Above: Kenelm Lee Guinness was favoured to win the 1922 TT after his 1914 victory, but his Sunbeam ran two bearings on the day before the race. It was repaired, but then developed clutch trouble just before the start. Here 'KLG' talks with his mechanic, W. F. Perkins, both of them unaware of the impending anti-climax.

17

Raincoats again: officials watch as Jean Chassagne and his mechanic manoeuvre their 2-litre four-cylinder Sunbeam before the start of the 500-mile 1922 French Grand Prix at Strasbourg. The horseshoe on the radiator brought no luck, for the entire three-car team of Sunbeams vacated the race with broken inlet valves.

Another British race, however, the RAC Tourist Trophy, or 'TT', was firmly 'on' in the Isle of Man. Last held there in 1914, the 1922 event betrayed the RAC's astonishing insularity at the time; instead of adopting the new 2-litre Formula they adhered to the old 1921 rules allowing cars of up to 3 litres.

The result was that just nine cars, all British, were entered, Sunbeam being happy to employ the redundant 'Talbot' straight-eight Grand Prix cars with Sunbeam radiators, while the young Bentley marque prepared three racing editions of their 3-litre sports model. As for Vauxhall, assuming the 3-litre rules would apply to other races, they went to the great expense and trouble of building three brand new 3-litre four-cylinder twin ohc cars, blissfully unaware that these would be obsolete after the TT, except for minor home events at Brooklands etc.

Neck and neck: midway during the 1922 French Grand Prix, Bugatti driver Pierre de Vizcaya, on the right, comes up to pass Giulio Foresti's ugly barrel-bodied Ballot. But the fiery Italian resists, and the pair slam past the tribunes abreast of each other. Vizcaya eventually finished second, but Foresti's car broke a piston.

For identification purposes the RAC required that the Sunbeams be painted blue-grey, the Vauxhalls red and the Bentleys cream, this at a time when other major events stipulated national racing colours — green for Britain, blue for France, red for Italy, blue and white for the USA, and white for Germany. The race was

held in wet, misty conditions, over the famous 37¾-mile motor-cycle course, Chassagne in a Sunbeam winning from a Bentley and a Vauxhall, with two more Bentleys following in to clinch the team prize (an item not provided but hastily purchased in Douglas after the race!). A 1500 cc race run concurrently was won by the inevitable Talbot-Darracqs, with A. Lee Guinness and A. Divo first and second. Frenchman Moriceau inverted the third car spectacularly, giving third place to a Bugatti. The relative isolation of the Isle of Man and the miserable weather kept attendance down to a few thousand, and after this unsuccessful race the TT became dormant for several more years.

A SPORTS CAR GRAND PRIX

The Belgians were luckier in promoting their Grand Prix. The title 'Belgian Grand Prix' was used before World War 1 for a combined speed/regularity event, but this was the first real race. It was run for 3-litre touring cars rather than 2-litre racers, and the circuit used lay between Spa and Francorchamps, near the German frontier. First used in 1921 for a motorcycle Grand Prix, it possessed many twists, turns and gradients in a lap length of 8¾ miles. Fortuitously, the first Belgian car Grand Prix produced sunny weather and an all-Belgian victory, with Belgian driver Baron de Tornaco winning in an interesting car called an Imperia-Abadal. This was a 3-litre 16-valve 'four' built in Belgium to an advanced Spanish design, and it beat a Chenard-Walcker and a 2-litre Bignan, while a trio of FNs, another home marque, took the 1½-litre class and the team prize.

Following the Corsican example, that Belgian race was the second to apply the term 'Grand Prix' to an event not conforming with the current Grand Prix Formula. The French, and the

Aston Martin of Britain elected to run two 1½-litre twin-cam voiturettes in the 2-litre 1922 French GP. Clive Gallop in car No. 8, here being refuelled, was up to sixth place by half-distance, but both cars eventually retired with magneto trouble.

The first massed start in Grand Prix racing, at Strasbourg in 1922, on roads muddy after early morning rain. Felice Nazzaro, who won the Grand Prix in 1907, and wins this race too, leads in his 2-litre six-cylinder Fiat.

19

Right: His lovely red Fiat is covered in Strasbourg mud, but the victorious Nazzaro and his mechanic look fairly fresh after over 6¼ hours of intensive motoring at an average of 79.2 mph. Three Bugattis were the only other cars left on the circuit, second man de Vizcaya being 58 minutes behind.

De Hane Segrave in an ailing Sunbeam soon to retire is passed by Count Giulio Masetti's Ballot on the long run past the pits at Strasbourg, watched by spectators massed in their thousands.

august ACF in particular, were a little piqued at such liberties with a title originally exclusive to their own classic race, but could do little about it. The subsequent 1922 Grand Prix saw their pique deflected to their own manufacturers; after having to stomach America's 1921 victory, their cars were now defeated by Italy's Fiats!

The race had been moved from Le Mans to a new road course at Strasbourg, and five marques contributed new 2-litre cars. Rolland-Pilain and Bugatti of France both fielded straight-eights, both coincidentally having hydraulic front brakes *à la*

1921 Duesenberg. Ballot of France and Sunbeam of Britain had new 'fours', and Fiat three lovely little 'sixes' which outpaced everyone right from the massed start—the first ever employed in a Grand Prix. Unhappily the predominant Italian trio was drastically reduced to one car when a too-closely machined rear axle failed and wheels flew, first from Biagio Nazzaro's car, the resulting crash killing the driver, and then from Bordino's car while he was in the lead. Thus veteran Felice Nazzaro, Biagio's uncle, had to consider himself lucky to win by an hour from two Bugattis, the only other finishers in a race further marred, like the TT, by rain and muddy roads.

Ballot, clearly losing their touch, produced three 'streamlined' cars with bloated circular bodies of grisly aspect and disappointing performance, while the Bugattis bore somewhat less ugly 'barrel' bodies. The British Sunbeams were faster, but all three retired with the same defect (broken inlet valves), while a pair of 1½-litre Aston Martins also dropped out.

Above: Piccioni and Rougier in two of the sleek 4-litre six-cylinder sleeve-valve Voisins which dominated the Touring Grand Prix which followed the 1922 French GP. These cars, designed by Gabriel Voisin, former aircraft manufacturer and aerodynamicist, defeated the Peugeot and Bignan opposition, Rougier and Duray, veterans from the 'Heroic Age' of racing, occupying the first two places, with the other Voisins third and fifth.

While modern Sunbeams failed in the Grand Prix, older ones upheld the marque's reputation in lesser spheres. This 1912 3-litre Coupe de l'Auto model won the Duke of York Long Handicap at the Essex MC's Royal meeting at Brooklands in 1922, driven by the English girl Miss Ivy Cummings, who averaged 83.5 mph.

Big names: Pietro Bordino, winner of the 1922 Italian GP at the new Monza track, is met by Fascist leader Benito Mussolini, a keen enthusiast for motor racing, and destined to become Il Duce of Italy a month later. On the right is the Fiat president Giovanni Agnelli.

Bird's eye view of the 1922 Monza-type 1½-litre twin ohc Chiribiri voiturette racer, showing restricted space for the riding mechanic.

On the day after the Grand Prix, the Strasbourg course 'hosted' another long-distance race for up to 3-litre touring four-seaters, called the Touring Grand Prix. Run over 443¾ miles, with a fuel allowance of 16.6 mpg, this focused further attention on the new sporting car category and attracted eleven starters. These comprised four Voisins and three Peugeots, all with sleeve-valve engines, three Bignans with desmodromic (positively closed) valve gear, and an AM. A new starting system was devised, with the drivers standing alongside their cars, jumping aboard at flag-fall, starting their engines by electric starter, and setting off.

With low fuel consumption of vital importance, getaways were scarcely electrifying, but the Voisins soon revealed remarkable speed, outpacing all opposition to score a 1-2-3 victory. The AM caught fire with 26 gallons of fuel aboard and burnt to a cinder, and André Boillot in his Peugeot caused annoyance by slipstreaming the Voisins in an effort to keep up. The Voisins, product of Gabriel Voisin, renowned aircraft builder, gave an admirable lesson in the value of good aerodynamics; they had clean streamlined bodywork and disc-covered wheels, and finished with nearly 2 gallons of fuel left in their tanks.

A further variation on the touring car racing theme was pioneered that same season on a narrow little course in the St Germain forest east of Paris. This was the Bol d'Or ('golden bowl'), engineered by M. Eugène Mauve, which lasted 24 hours and was open to cars from 350 to 1100 cc, and also three-wheelers. Races lasting 24 hours had taken place in the USA since 1905, but this was the first in Europe. One driver alone was allowed during the 24 hours, although a riding mechanic was optional, even if unpopular for his weight, while rest periods totalling 4 hours were permitted. This gruelling endurance race, perpetuated in France today by a motorcycle event, was productive of many ingenious little vehicles, and some epic drives through the years. The first event, in 1922, resulted in victory for André Morel in a new French marque, the Amilcar, which narrowly beat two Salmsons.

Umbrella'd and hatted again (above), the Italian crowd at Monza watch the start of the Italian Grand Prix on a wet track. The meteoric Bordino has already gone by, and Nazzaro in Fiat No. 5 here leads de Vizcaya, in the sole Bugatti running, and a Diatto.

Alfieri Maserati (below) was an enterprising and successful builder and driver of racing cars before he and his brothers founded their own marque. With the Isotta-Fraschini special here he won the 1922 Circuit of Mugello by over 2 minutes from Count Brilli-Peri's Fiat. The car had a four-cylinder single ohc engine utilizing one block from a Hispano-Suiza V8 aero-engine.

THE 'BAD ROADS RACE'

Another surprising race was inaugurated during that fruitful season. Like many other clubs, the AC du Nord in northern France wanted to promote a race but lacked a suitable circuit. Instead they ingeniously exploited the badly war-torn roads around Lille, announcing a race comprising 'a test of suspension and holding-of-the-road', to be called the *Circuit des Routes Pavées,* or colloquially the 'Bad Roads Race'. The 8¼-mile course, based on Pont-à-Marq, was narrow, abounding in ill-laid pavé, with loose flints or slimy mud on each side, while an artificial cobble-stone ridge 10 inches high was laid across the road by the main spectator stand, followed by a crude level-crossing with projecting rails and a deep gulley. Sixty-one cars from 750 cc to 4½ litres took part, sporting many ingenious varieties of hydraulic, pneumatic, leaf spring and rubber suspension.

Rain added to the drivers' difficulties, several cars visiting bordering ditches, while two overturned and one charged a tree, the starting handle being driven hard into the trunk. A woman driver, Mme Violette Morriss, won the 750 cc class with a spidery Benjamin, and other class 'firsts' fell to Salmson, Voisin, Bignan, La Ponette, Berliet, Chenard-Walcker, Peugeot and Farman, Lagache (Chenard-Walcker) being fastest at a 42 mph average.

Rain figured all too prominently in 1922 motor racing, never more so than at the Italian Grand Prix meeting. Here again there

No race was more redolent of 1920s conditions than the Targa Florio, run over several gruelling 67.2-mile laps in primitive Sicilian mountain country. Such rugged going demanded rugged cars and drivers, exemplified by the burly Giuseppe Campari and his riding mechanic Fugazza, in a 6.1-litre Type 40-60 Alfa, built in 1914, but still going strong in 1922.

was a change of circuit, the 1921 Brescia triangle being abandoned in favour of the all-new purpose-built track in the former Royal park at Monza, outside Milan. Monza's existence was a veritable *tour de force*. Italian bureaucracy did its utmost to foil the AC di Milano's bold aims to build a permanent race circuit, vetting the cutting-down of trees and the use of explosives, filtering plans through numerous obstructive authorities, and even posting guards to ensure that no unauthorized work was carried out. Despite this the club pressed on, and eventually the municipality capitulated before such enthusiasm, and the combined track-cum-road course, 10 km (6.2 miles) round and shaped like a double loop, was completed in an astonishing 110 days.

'Monza week' was booked for early September 1922, with two main races for 1½ and 2 litres held a week apart. For the first time in Europe, substantial cash prizes were offered, totalling 150,000 lire for the voiturette race and 300,000 lire for the Grand Prix, plus bonuses for records set and numerous trophies. So much effort deserved greater success. Of sixty-two entries received for the two races, only seventeen cars started, although this did not diminish crowds estimated to exceed 220,000 during the seven days.

For the *Gran Premio di Vetturette*, which had nine starters, Fiat had taken a leaf out of Talbot-Darracq's book and produced a 1500 cc four-cylinder 8-valve racer from half their obsolete 1921 3-litre straight-eights. These fleet little cars just ran away with the race, during which it rained heavily, Pietro Bordino leading their 1-2-3-4 formation at 83.1 mph, with a Chiribiri and two 'Sascha' Austro-Daimlers designed by Dr Porsche panting home an hour and more behind. The *Gran Premio* was a near-repetition; there were eight starters, it rained, and Bordino again dominated the event in his six-cylinder 2-litre Fiat, winning at 86.89 mph.

In his brother's footsteps: André Boillot, younger brother of the great Georges who was killed in the Great War, took up his mantle in the Peugeot team with much success. With this 3.8-litre sleeve-valve car he won the 1922 Florio Cup race (a separate event from the Targa), by a margin of 1 hour 6 mins, from Segrave's 5-litre Sunbeam.

An old hand in new territory: Christian Lautenschlager, the winner of the 1908 and 1914 French Grands Prix, driving his 1914 4½-litre Mercedes in the 1922 Targa Florio. His tenth place indicated that he had lost his fire; a similar Mercedes driven by Masetti won the race outright 27 minutes ahead of the old master from Stuttgart.

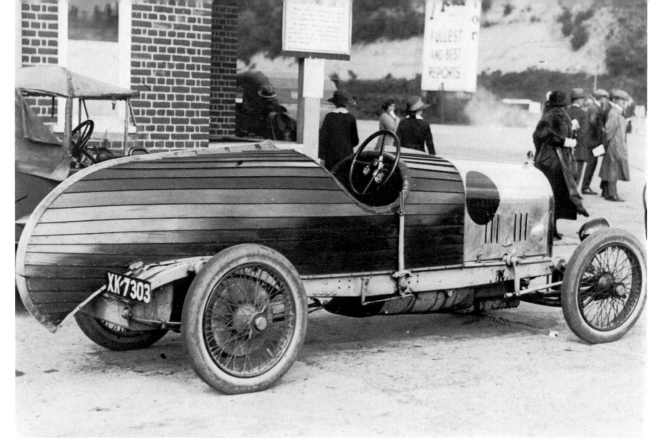

Literally boat-bodied, this curious clinker-built two-seater 3-litre Bentley was raced at the BARC's 1922 Whitsun meeting at Brooklands by its owner, the Hon. G. A. Egerton.

Nazzaro, that year's French Grand Prix winner, was second in another Fiat, and de Viscaya's straight-eight 'barrel' Bugatti third and last, running on wheels and tyres borrowed from Fiat! Four Bugattis had arrived, but practice showed that their axle ratios were incorrect. Lacking spares, all were withdrawn, but to prevent too much of a walkover Fiat accordingly lent a set of wheels for one Bugatti, thereby adding some much-needed interest to the race. After the Fiats finished, the effervescent crowd invaded the track, establishing a precedent prevalent at Monza to this day.

During practice an Austro-Daimler driver, Kuhn, had overturned on one of Monza's low bankings and been killed; the Austrian team had then been withdrawn from the Grand Prix. Two German six-cylinder Heims ran rather hopelessly and

A Briton abroad: Londoner Jack E. Scales went out to Italy before the Great War, racing motorcycles and then cars, and working for Fiat and later Chiribiri. This picture shows him winning the 1½-litre class of the 1922 21.2-mile Aosta-Grand St Bernard mountain climb in a works Chiribiri.

retired, as did two Diattos, one driven by Alfieri Maserati. This driver figured in another Monza race, the Autumn Grand Prix, a month later, taking the 3-litre class for Diatto. He also won the Mugello race and two major Italian hillclimbs with an Isotta-Fraschini 'special' he had constructed, employing one bank of an Hispano-Suiza V8 aero-engine; clearly Maserati was a name to reckon with in the future.

The rain which fell so generously in the Isle of Man and at Strasbourg, Pont-à-Marq and Monza also fell at the second Avus meeting in Germany, where a sure-footed newcomer named Rudolf Caracciola placed fourth in a 1.1-litre Fafnir behind three bigger cars. Rain fell, too, at Le Mans, turning the 1100 cc Cyclecar Grand Prix into a mudbath, from which Benoist (Salmson) emerged the winner, but it spared the Grand Prix des

Patron of the future: the young man is G. A. (Tony) Vandervell, destined over 30 years later to found the highly successful British Vanwall Formula 1 team, but here in a Ford Model T-based, ohv-headed single-seater 'special' before the BARC's Easter meeting at Brooklands in 1922. He had to retire from his race after three laps.

Sometimes called 'the Rolls-Royce of Austria', but more widely known as the make of car in which Archduke Ferdinand was assassinated in 1914, precipitating the First World War, the Vienna-built Graf & Stift of the 1920s was a large 7.7-litre six-cylinder car able to perform creditably in Continental hillclimbs. The scene is Semmering in 1922, and the driver is Dipl. Ing. Josef Graf himself, who won his class.

27

A rare French invention (right) was the Circuit des Routes Pavées *or 'Bad Roads Race', inaugurated in 1922 on war-torn roads outside Lille as a test for speed, stamina and suspension. This Salmson competing in the 1923 race is leaping the artificial ramp laid on the cobbled finishing straight to add to the hazards and discomfort.*

Driver/manufacturer Robert Sénéchal takes the same ramp in the Ruby-engined Sénéchal with which he won the 750 cc class from three Peugeot Quadrilettes. This race was an admirable test for shock absorbers, snubbers and other aids to suspension, and also marked the first use in a race of low-pressure 'balloon' tyres.

Voiturettes on the same circuit, where Kenelm Lee Guinness, creator of the KLG sparking plug, did the winning in a Talbot-Darracq. It was Guinness and Talbot-Darracq who won again in a miraculously dry 200 Miles Race at Brooklands, where his team-mate Chassagne suffered a burst tyre and careered straight over the banking without harm to driver or mechanic, although the former's shoes were left neatly on the track, to the mystification of passing drivers.

A revealing insight into the problems of travelling to distant motor races in those pre-airliner days was provided by Guinness, who owned a converted trawler called *The Ocean Rover*. With a voiturette race in Spain and a big car race in Sicily, both in early November, it was decided to take the cars (three 1½-litre Talbot-Darracqs and two 4.9-litre Sunbeams) by boat, together with *chef d'equipe* Louis Coatalen, drivers and mechanics. A very

rough Biscay crossing left them somewhat jaded for the Penya Rhin Grand Prix in Spain, but the usual Talbot-Darracq victory was duly scored by Guinness, with an Aston Martin and a Chiribiri unexpectedly interposing between his and the next Talbot. This was Segrave's car, which broke an inlet valve and thereafter staged a series of engine fires which made driving very uncomfortable. 'Put your feet in a puddle if they get too hot' was Coatalen's unsympathetic advice!

Sailing on to Sicily, Segrave and Chassagne then drove the big Sunbeams in the Coppa Florio, a separate race that year from the Targa, but on the same gruelling mountain circuit. A somewhat naïve Segrave went practising in late afternoon and was caught by a heavy rainstorm and then by sudden nightfall. He and his mechanic had to sleep out in a barn, but in the race they finished second to Boillot's sleeve-valve Peugeot, despite persistent plug trouble and a broken frame cross member. Chassagne with the other car lost all his oil when a flying stone severed an oil pipe, but he refilled with olive oil obtained in a remote village and was still running when the race ended.

Sensation of the 1923 French Grand Prix was the team of supercharged 2-litre eight-cylinder Fiats, which were driven from the Turin factory over the Alps to the Tours circuit for the race. Pietro Bordino has just arrived, and this street-side view emphasizes the sleek low lines of the cars.

'Le Tank': Ettore Bugatti surprised the French at Tours with his short, stubby 'tank'-bodied 2-litre straight-eights with full-width streamlined bodies. This one, driven by Friedrich, finished a good third.

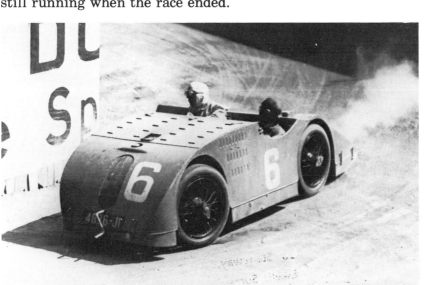

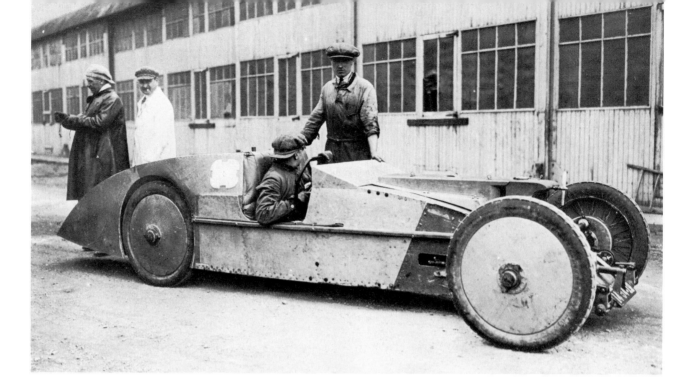

BRITAIN'S TURN

Seeking something for nothing: obliged to use a six-cylinder sleeve-valve engine of relatively low output, Gabriel Voisin sought to offset it by aerodynamic means, with this bizarre bodywork built in aeronautical semi-monocoque fashion from wood and aluminium sheeting. Of the three cars, only one survived the 497-mile race, taking fifth place.

In contrast with 1922, the big races in 1923 were all sunshine, both physically and metaphorically, especially for a Britain which had not won a major motor race since 1912 and was getting rather anxious. Yet the success she achieved, aided by good luck, was more gratifying to lay patriots than to those 'in the know'. Marking Fiat's sweeping success in two 1922 classics with their six-cylinder car, Louis Coatalen decided that Sunbeam, too, needed a six-cylinder racer, and forthwith hired one of the Fiat design team, Vincent Bertarione, to produce it. So closely did the resultant Sunbeams resemble the 1922 Fiat that they were dubbed 'Fiats in green paint'.

Coatalen came from Brittany, so was presumably untroubled by this national slur; he wanted Sunbeam the marque to win a

Britain wins: Henry O'Neal De Hane Segrave slams past the stands at Tours in the 2-litre six-cylinder Sunbeam with which he won the 1923 French Grand Prix, with other Sunbeams second and fourth. Although outpaced at first by the supercharged straight-eight Fiats, the British cars gained a famous victory through high speed reliability.

Grand Prix, and by those unforeseen circumstances that make motor racing so excitingly uncertain he achieved this. Ironically, for *their* 1923 Grand Prix design Fiat reverted to the straight-eight, but with a decisive difference — they supercharged it. Not only Coatalen but all designers studied rival designs, then as now, and Fiat engineers undoubtedly took close heed of two supercharged 1½-litre Mercedes which had performed somewhat indifferently in the 1922 Targa Florio. It was the principle, not the application, that interested them, and instead of employing a Roots 'figure of eight' double-rotor type of compressor they opted for a vane-type design patented by the German brothers Wittig.

The 1923 French Grand Prix was held over a 14.18-mile triangular circuit at Tours. Surprisingly, the three new Fiats were *driven* there, over the Alps from Turin, although it is unlikely that their superchargers were used, a hinged flap in effect 'decompressing' them even though the blowers remained permanently engaged. When the drivers Bordino, Salamano and Giaccone gave their fierce red mounts their full head *con compressore* on the Tours straights, however, they left the French and British opposition very satisfyingly behind, and the opening stages of the race saw the great Bordino flying out ahead, while the other Fiats lay in wait and bickered with the Sunbeams.

Then Fate took over; eighty-four miles and the leading Fiat stammered, slowed, and stopped. Half-distance and Giaccone's car also failed. Then, with four laps to go and leading, Salamano's Fiat, too, broke down; all three engines choked on the unfiltered dust pumped in by their superchargers. So Sunbeam the emulators triumphed over Fiat the innovators, and romped home 1-2-4 in the 496½-mile race in the order Segrave, Divo, Guinness.

At their HQ at the Hotel du Boeuf Couronné in the village of Neuvy-le-Roi, the Sunbeam racing mechanics take a break from race preparation. Holding the donkey's ears is Segrave's mechanic Dutoit. Car No. 2 is Guinness's, which came fourth.

Réné Thomas demonstrates his own strength and the lightness of the cylinder block of the new twelve-cylinder 2-litre Delage which made its début at Tours. It retired with its petrol tank pierced by a stone.

Adding to the many design innovations of the fruitful 1923 racing season, the Benz concern of Mannheim, Germany, sent a team of rear-engined cars with 2-litre twin ohc six-cylinder engines and rear swing axles to the Grand Prix of Europe at Monza. Ferdinando Minoia, who was running fourth at the finish, makes a pit stop; note that his riding mechanic has a side door!

Never was there a race like that at Tours for technical novelties. Third home was a Bugatti, one of four with 2-litre eight-cylinder engines in unmanageably short chassis carrying ugly 'tank' style full-width bodies of approximate aerofoil profile. The fifth-place Voisin, sole survivor of four, had a 2-litre six-cylinder sleeve-valve engine in a semi-monocoque chassis of combined wood and aluminium sheet, with streamlining as curious and unlovely as on the Bugattis. A single Delage which retired early had a vee-twelve cylinder four ohc engine of formidable complexity and potential, whereas of three Rolland-Pilains which looked faster than they were one had a six-cylinder cuff-valve engine while the others had twin ohc straight-eights; all retired.

SUPERCHARGING AT INDIANAPOLIS

'Supercharging' was a new word spoken elsewhere with bated breath that momentous season. Two months before the Grand Prix the Indianapolis 500 had been run to 2-litre rules for the first time, attracting European entries. A Mercedes three-car entry was a major surprise from a Germany then grappling with inflation on a terrifying scale (where a loaf of bread cost 100 marks in the morning and 100,000 in the afternoon, and £1 sterling was worth 100 million marks). These trim white 'Mercs' had 2-litre four-cylinder two ohc 16-valve engines with roller main and big end bearings and mercury-cooled exhaust valves, but the vertical Roots superchargers were their greatest novelty.

These were engaged through a clutch when the throttle pedal was fully depressed, and in action down the Indianapolis straights they produced a memorably penetrating shriek coupled

One-armed leader: Pietro Bordino, his left arm injured after a practice crash, pluckily leads the Grand Prix of Europe at Monza in the straight-eight Roots-supercharged Fiat, his mechanic changing gear for him.

Left: exhausted and melancholy, Pietro Bordino seen in the pits at Monza with Ing. Guido Fornaca after having to withdraw from the European Grand Prix when leading at half-distance. Fiat still won the race, however, Carlo Salamano taking first place, closely followed by his team-mate Felice Nazzaro.

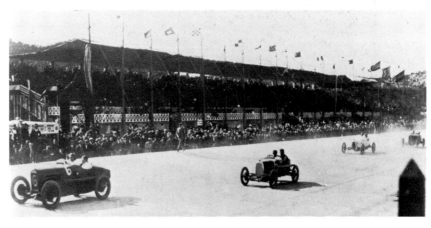

with impressive speed. At half-distance Werner's Mercedes lay a strong third, but eventually troubles set in and eighth and eleventh were the Germans' best placings. The 1923 '500' also marked the end of body restrictions and brought a flood of lean, elegant single-seaters by Duesenberg and Miller. Harry Miller built his cars for sale to other teams, and the reprehensible American habit of naming cars after their sponsors began. Thus the race was won by Tommy Milton driving an 'HCS Special' which was really a Miller, followed by three 'Durants' which were also Millers, and a 'Barber-Warnock' which was a Ford.

Supercharging had to succeed at some time, but its first real success in Europe went unheralded and unsung. Twenty-nine days after Indianapolis and four before the French Grand Prix, a single 1½-litre four-cylinder Fiat driven by the veteran Cagno

won the Vetturette Grand Prix on the old 1921 Brescia circuit. This was a very 'national' event, with no foreign entries — just OMs, Bianchis, Bugattis, Chiribiris — and the one Fiat, with engineer Vittorio Jano and an unusual number of Fiat executives in attendance.

With their younger drivers already practising with the supercharged 2-litre cars at Tours, Fiat induced the veteran Alessandro Cagno — winner of the first Targa Florio race in 1906 — to drive the *vetturetta* in this discreet try-out. He performed his task in exemplary manner, taking a lead he never lost; he lapped at 86.75 mph and won the 324-mile road race at 80.14 mph, over half an hour ahead of a Bugatti and a Chiribiri. History does not relate whether this first supercharged Fiat had a Wittig or Roots-type blower, but contemporary use of the former at Tours would suggest that it also served in the Brescia race, the first in Europe to be won by a supercharged car.

Fiats made no fuss about this successful little foray; the failure at Tours obsessed them more, and they set to without delay to remedy the problem. The Wittig compressors were replaced by Roots-type, with careful filtering after the French disaster. Their next battleground was the all-important Italian Grand Prix, which for 1923 was also termed the first European Grand Prix in an effort to impart extra status. The mercurial Bordino ('the fastest driver in Europe' in H. O. D. Segrave's view) looked all set to balance out his Tours disappointment, when his Fiat shed a wheel during practice and overturned. Bordino damaged his wrist, but Giaccone, riding with him, was killed.

Below left: real roads, and rough ones at that, in the 1923 Penya Rhin Grand Prix, held on the Villafranca circuit. Dario Resta (Talbot) leads an Elizalde and Zborowski's Aston Martin. The gruelling 321.6-mile race was won by Albert Divo (Talbot) from Zborowski and Resta.

Below: a welcome walk to the victory reception by the 1923 French Grand Prix winners, Segrave the driver and Dutoit the mechanic, after being confined within their Sunbeam's cockpit for over 6½ hours.

35

The San Sebastian circuit in the Basque region of Northern Spain was introduced in 1923, when two French straight-eight Rolland-Pilains won the first two places, despite their drivers suffering from food poisoning. Guyot, the winner, leads the opening lap from Delalandre and Haimovici's Ballot; note the rough, unmetalled road forming the finishing straight.

Bordino pluckily contested the race with his arm in plaster, his mechanic changing gear for him, but with Fiat chief Agnelli's persuasion he eventually gave up, leaving the Fiat 1-2 victory to Salamano and Nazzaro. Interestingly, three American eight-cylinder Millers took part, one driven by Jimmy Murphy, the 1921 Grand Prix winner, finishing third. Even more interestingly, lying fourth and fifth when the crowd performed their customary invasion of the track were two German Benz cars of radical design. Anticipating the Auto Unions of 1934–39 and all modern racing cars, these had their engines (twin-cam 'sixes') behind the driver and ahead of the rear axle, which was independently suspended by swinging half-shafts and quarter-elliptic springs, although a rigid front axle was used.

A second Monza death during practice resulted in three important non-starters. These were new Alfa Romeos designated the Tipo P1, with six-cylinder twin ohc unsupercharged engines. They were manifestly outpaced by the blown Fiats in practice, and when the works driver Ugo Sivocci crashed in one and was killed, Alfa Romeo withdrew the team from the European Grand Prix. Their day was yet to come.

The busy round got busier. Spain contributed two new Grands Prix, one at San Sebastian, the other at Sitges near Barcelona. The San Sebastian Grand Prix was run over a long and difficult road course measuring 11.03 miles per lap, but the race was poorly supported, only Rolland-Pilain sending proper Grand Prix

cars along. Before the race their drivers Guyot and the veteran Héméry both suffered food poisoning, and Héméry had to hand his car over to Delalandre, his mechanic. Guyot was so ill that he had to stop during the race, Haimovici in a 2-litre Ballot taking the lead. Guyot recovered sufficiently to resume driving, catching the Ballot to win, while Delalandre also got by to complete Rolland-Pilain's only Grand Prix success.

Not Brooklands but the Sitges banked speedway near Barcelona, Spain. Count Louis Zborowski takes his American straight-eight Miller high up when leading the 1923 Grand Prix. A burst tyre 2 laps from the finish robbed him of victory.

The most significant mechanical development in 1923 motor racing was the advent of supercharging in Europe, initially on the 1½-litre four-cylinder Fiat which won the Brescia voiturette Grand Prix on its first appearance. This photograph, taken later in 1923, shows the compressor at the front end of the crankcase.

A smoke screen from Parry Thomas's Marlborough before the start of the 1923 200 Miles Race at Brooklands fails to hide the two formidable supercharged Fiats. No. 32 is Carlo Salamano's car, while close to Chronograph Villa can be seen No. 26, driven by Malcolm Campbell.

Fiat fiasco: after leading the 200 Miles by an ever increasing margin the two Italian cars were out after 13 laps with dire engine trouble. Campbell's white-bonneted car leaves ample evidence below of mechanical ills; Salamano, goggles on forehead, gazes glumly at the engine, watched by Hugh P. McConnell, interpreter and joint race organizer.

The Sitges event had dramas of another kind. The brand new course was a short, sharply banked affair in concrete, 1½ miles to the lap and proclaimed 'the most emotional speedway in the world'. A grandiose opening meeting in October was attended by the enthusiastic King Alfonso, the programme comprising the first Spanish Grand Prix for 2-litre cars, plus 1½-litre and 1100 cc supporting events. As at San Sebastian, entries were poor. STD sent two Sunbeams for the Grand Prix and two Talbots for the 1500 cc race, scoring a 'double'. Divo the former mechanic won the Spanish Grand Prix, but as with Segrave at Tours fortune was with him, for the dashing Count Louis Zborowski in his straight-eight Miller was leading the 248½-mile race with two laps to go when a tyre burst, letting the Sunbeam past to win. It was certainly STD's lucky day; Talbot took 1–2 in the 1500 cc event, Resta leading Divo home to register the marque's fourth consecutive win that season.

M. Coatalen's anxiety to maintain Talbot's reputation of never losing a race possibly cost them a fifth victory, even though it added greatly to the interest in the 1923 200 Miles Race. After Cagno's encouraging success at Brescia, Fiat decided to send two supercharged '1500s' to the British race on 13 October. Eight days later came the Penya Rhin Grand Prix, so Coatalen decided not to risk an encounter with the fleet Italian cars, and opted for Spain.

The race before the race: mechanics hard at work preparing the two 12/50 four-cylinder ohv Alvises of C. M. Harvey and H. H. Brayshaw for the 1923 200 Miles race. Harvey's car had been seriously damaged by fire five days before the race, but the extra work of repairing it was richly rewarded; with the departure of the Fiats, Harvey moved up to score a non-stop victory at 93.29 mph, while Brayshaw finished eighth—an unexpected but most welcome success for the young British marque.

'To sleep, perchance to dream'?—or is the mechanic in Klöble's 1½-litre Type 5/15 NSU taking his instruction to get down out of the wind too conscientiously? The event is the 138-mile Avusrennen of 1923, won by Klöble at 74.23 mph, with two other NSUs closely following.

Driving a 1½-litre AC stripped of everything strippable, and using a tiny fuel tank, J. A. Joyce broke the Brooklands Test Hill record in November 1923, climbing in 8.28 secs. This knocked 0.21 secs. off Frazer Nash's record with a GN, achieved 12 months earlier.

FIATS FAIL!

Without the Talbots there was nothing to challenge the blown Fiats, and an Italian walkover was anticipated. Odds on a win for Salamano were evens, with 3:1 for Campbell and Harvey (Alvis) next favoured at only 10:1. Astonishingly, after both had lapped at over 100 mph, the Fiats broke down, Salamano on lap 12 and Campbell a lap later, both with suspected piston failure leading to broken connecting rods. That left the race wide open to the British cars, and C. M. Harvey's pushrod ohv Alvis 12/50 with track body won at a splendid 93.29 mph from a Bugatti, an AC and an Aston Martin.

Even the humble Austin Seven, just introduced as a utilitarian baby car, went motor racing. A. C. Waite first won a race at Brooklands, then went all the way to Monza for the 155-mile Cyclecar Grand Prix, winning the 750 cc class from an Anzani and a GL. At the 200 Miles at Brooklands, E. Gordon England in another 750 cc Austin cheekily finished second to a factory Salmson in the 1100 cc event. British cars were certainly on the 'up and up', as also became evident in a very significant new French race.

Right down to it: Robert Benoist and his mécano *almost sacrifice visibility in their efforts to help the circa 34 bhp of their twin-cam Salmson, while winning the 186-mile 1100 cc Cyclecar GP at Monza in 1923. Bueno in a similar car was second and made the fastest lap at 69.04 mph.*

Mountain climbing was a Continental speciality since the early days of motor racing, Mont Ventoux in the French Alpes Maritimes being a popular French venue since 1902. With a course 13½ miles in length, it resembled a short road race rather than the brief sprint of the average British hillclimb. Seen on one of the unmade turns in the 1923 event is Réné Thomas, making FTD for the second consecutive year with one of the two 5-litre six-cylinder Delages constructed for such events.

It may be forgotten now, but the original title of the Le Mans 24 Hours race was the Rudge-Whitworth Cup. The idea for an endurance race through day and night for the new competition-type 'touring' cars is attributed jointly to M. Emile Coquille, Paris manager for Rudge-Whitworth, wire wheel and motorcycle makers, engineer/journalist Charles Faroux, and Georges Durand of the Le Mans-based AC de l'Ouest. Doubtless the success of the 1922 Bol d'Or 24-hour race spurred them on, and Coquille's offer of 100,000 francs (say £4000) clinched the birth of what has since become the world's most famous motor race.

Faroux and Durand worked out the rules, admitting 'tourers of fast sporting type' with four seats and ballast equivalent to three passengers, only the driver actually being aboard. In effect the race constituted the first of three annual rounds for the Rudge-Whitworth Triennial Cup, one of those baffling handicap formulae beloved by the French being drawn up to determine the winner. To the public, fortunately, the winner is the first home and hence the fastest, but the Rudge Cup contest persisted up to World War 2, and was succeeded by the modern Index of Performance.

Realizing that watching the repeated passage of cars being driven to last twice round the clock could pall with spectators, the AC de l'Ouest laid on several extra entertainments. These included an evening fireworks display, dancing, wireless concerts, a jazz band, a cinema, an American bar and a fair, thus inaugurating the famous *Village*. The course was the famous Sarthe triangle as used for the 1921 Grand Prix, rather narrow and tree-lined, and measuring 10¾ miles per lap. French Army searchlights illuminated two corners, and acetylene lamps served elsewhere to augment the cars' own headlights.

The entry was heavily French, with thirty-one home products ranged against one Belgian Excelsior and one British 3-litre Bentley. Some of 1922's rain was reserved for the first half of the race, washing out the promised fireworks and soaking the public. The Bentley, privately owned, entered and driven by John F. Duff, with F. C. Clement of Bentleys as co-driver, provided the main opposition. Ever a spur to the Chenards, Bignans, Lorraines and other French marques, it made a bid for the lead on the second day when the rain had stopped, breaking the lap record three times but running out of fuel when one of Le Mans' famous stones holed the tank. Repairs took 2½ hours, and the British car eventually finished behind two Chenard-Walckers and two Bignans in a modest fifth place. Le Mans and Bentley, however, had made their mark. . . .

Rudi Who? An unknown 22-year-old Rhinelander, Rudolf Caracciola, after winning the 1100 cc class race at the Berlin Stadium at Charlottenberg in 1923. The car, on loan from its owner Fritz Wusthoff, is a 4/14 1016 cc four-cylinder Ego built by the former Merkur aircraft factory, and Caracciola's win earned him a dozen free lunches and several thousand marks at a time of chronic inflation. During the next 16 years he was to gain 25 Grand Prix victories and innumerable hillclimb wins.

Enzo Ferrari finds time to look at the photographer, but the other Alfa Romeo drivers, Giulio Masetti (in white), Ugo Sivocci and Antonio Ascari are too busy discussing the morrow's race— the 1923 Targa Florio. Sivocci won, Ascari was second and Masetti fourth in Alfa Romeo's first major race victory; the cars are six-cylinder Type RL derivatives with seven-bearing crankshafts. Note the marque's famous quadrifoglio *(four-leaf clover) symbol on the radiator cowling of No. 11.*

The enterprising Mr Duff had mixed luck again in the Spanish Touring Grand Prix at San Sebastian — yet another addition to the calendar. With 1½ laps to go he had a lead of nearly 10 miles on three larger Hispano-Suizas when a stone smashed his goggles and he hit a wall and retired. In token of his gallant drive Duff was awarded the 3-litre trophy anyway, there being no other finishers in the class. The new marque Bentley was certainly putting itself on the map.

* * *

3
GOLDEN AGE
1924-25

In 1924 Grand Prix racing reached a peak in brilliance and interest which would not be repeated for ten years, although it is to be doubted whether France or Fiat thought so. For the fifth successive time the French Grand Prix fell to a foreign marque, and France was *désolée*. For the second year running, the proud house of Fiat was defeated by a design usurped from their own drawing boards. This time the culprits were not Sunbeam but the up-and-coming Milanese marque Alfa Romeo, whose chief, Nicola Romeo, was determined to see his cars succeed in the highest class of motor racing.

Segrave's electrifying start with the supercharged 2-litre Sunbeam in the 1924 French Grand Prix at Lyons was later negatived by magneto trouble, and he could only finish fifth, but with the fastest lap at 76.7 mph. Behind him are Antonio Ascari (Alfa Romeo), and Divo (Delage), who finished second.

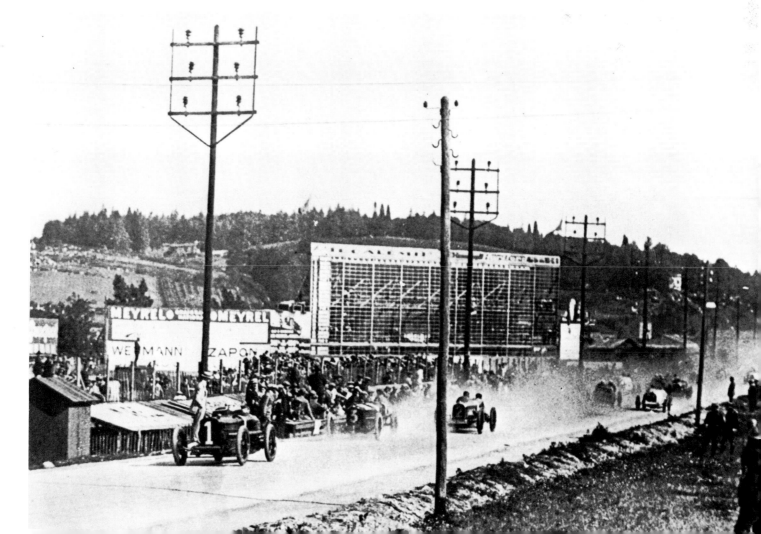

Their 1923 six-cylinder P1 design was woefully inferior to the fierce supercharged eight-cylinder Fiats, and Enzo Ferrari, at that time race-driving for Alfa Romeo, tells frankly in his book *My Terrible Joys* of how he persuaded the brilliant young engineer Vittorio Jano to leave Fiat and join Alfa Romeo. 'Snatch' was the expression he used, and 'snatched' Jano was. Whereas at Fiat, however, he was but one of a team, at Alfa Romeo he was given his head as chief designer, his first task being to produce a new Grand Prix car. Almost inevitably it was a supercharged straight-eight, following Fiat practice closely but improving upon it.

Called the P2, it proved immensely successful. As a last-minute entry it won its first 'try-out' race at Cremona, driven by Antonio Ascari, and it was Ascari who fought at Lyons in the 1924 French Grand Prix with the Sunbeams, Fiats and Delages, and held the lead with only two of the thirty-five laps to complete. Then he had to stop at the pits for water, after which the P2 refused to start. The cylinder head had cracked, but his mechanic Ramponi pushed until he dropped, and both men ended totally exhausted, lying on the roadside while Ascari's team-mate Campari went past to win the great race.

So the 'upstarts' from Milan won the first Grand Prix they ever contested, while the four Fiats which had taught them how to do it suffered dire brake troubles and all retired. As for the six-cylinder Sunbeams from England, with Roots superchargers

Uniquely beautiful, Bugatti's latest racing car, the 2-litre straight-eight Type 35, was a distinguished débutante in the 1924 Grand Prix. Though dogged by persistent tyre trouble, two finished in seventh and eighth positions, driven by Chassagne and Friedrich, who is seen here passing the stands.

Antonio Ascari in the new P2 eight-cylinder supercharged Alfa Romeo sweeps by with a commanding lead in the French Grand Prix. His was the only car of the team to have a cut-off stern with a spare wheel mounted upon it, the other Alfas wearing full-length tails. With 33 of the 35 laps accomplished, the situation for Ascari was to change dramatically.

fitted they were the fastest cars on the circuit. The luck that rode with them at Tours, however, forsook them at Lyons; a last-minute fitting of new magnetos proved disastrous, the green cars misfiring miserably in between bursts of speed, so that fifth place by Segrave, plus the record lap, was the best they could do.

The twelve-cylinder Delage which was too new at Tours was now *au point*, although running unsupercharged, and a trio of these cars finished an excellent second, third and sixth. As for Bugatti, his new cars were a cynosure for all appreciative eyes.

'Tyre bridges' at motor racing circuits are not a modern publicity device, as this 1924 Grand Prix picture shows. Passing underneath is Robert Benoist, erstwhile Salmson cyclecar driver and future European Champion, who finished third with one of the unsupercharged twelve-cylinder Delages.

The master of Molsheim had at last abandoned his eccentric experiments of 1922 and 1923, and produced five exquisite little unsupercharged 2-litre straight-eights for the Grand Prix. Apart from their sheer balanced beauty, these Type 35s were distinguished by their novel eight-spoke cast alloy wheels, although these, or the tyres specially made to suit them, caused the Bugattis' downfall at Lyons, where they could only finish seventh and eighth, last of the twenty starters to survive the 500½-mile race.

Clearly, supercharging had come to stay, even though some makers, Louis Delage and Ettore Bugatti in particular, were quite vehement about the 'unfairness' of the system. The Targa Florio early in the season had gone to Christian Werner on a supercharged Mercedes, one of the 1923 Indianapolis cars much improved by Dr Porsche. It was also unusual in being painted red rather than German white, the reason, it was suggested, being that armed bandits in the mountains were inclined to 'pot' at those cars not wearing Italian racing red! That 1924 race marked a peak in Targas, with 37 starters including teams from Fiat, Alfa Romeo and Itala of Italy, Mercedes and Aga from Germany, Steyr from Austria and Peugeot and Ballot from France.

Driving a 3.6-litre unblown Tipo RL Alfa with inspired devilry, Ascari wrested the lead from Werner on the last lap. A mere 50 yards from the finish, however, his engine seized solid, and while he and his mechanics struggled desperately to bring it to life again Werner tore past to win. The Sicilian crowd rushed irresistibly forward and pushed the Alfa bodily across the finishing line into second place, but then protests flew, up went the shout 'Squalifica!', and poor Ascari was disqualified for not finishing under his own power.

Ettore Bugatti's controversial aluminium alloy-spoked wheel, which first appeared on the Type 35 Bugattis at Lyons in 1924. The brake drums were cast integrally, but the rims were detachable, held in place by 24 countersunk screws. The team's tyre troubles in the race were attributed to inadequate vulcanizing of the special Dunlop racing tyres ordered by Bugatti and made at such short notice that they had to be flown to the Continent from Birmingham. Though much criticised as a result, subsequent events proved the excellence of the Bugatti alloy wheel.

ALFA ROMEO 1-2-3-4

Ascari won his third race, however, the Italian Grand Prix at Monza, without any question. Blasting his P2 into the lead, he never lost it, winning by 16 minutes at a prodigious 98.7 mph for the 497 miles. Behind him came Alfa after Alfa—Wagner, Campari and Minoia, in a sweeping Italian victory, with two cuff-valve Schmids 10 and 13 laps behind the victor, the only other finishers. Mercedes sent four new Porsche-designed straight-eight supercharged cars of advanced but immature design; these proved fast but unstable and tricky to handle, although Masetti actually worked up into second place among the Alfas by sheer skill and daring before fatigue and the sickness of his mechanic forced him back. Then the unfortunate Count Zborowski crashed his Mercedes at Lesmo and was killed, the other three German cars then being withdrawn.

Lamented non-starters at Monza were Fiat, although Bordino had practised and put in some good lap times. It was the end of the racing road for Italy's great champions, for apart from one isolated appearance in 1927 the proud Torinese marque never appeared again in European racing. Other absences were less excusable, a disappointing feature of 1924 races apart from the French Grand Prix being the curious inability of rival marques to meet each other. Delage, Sunbeam and Bugatti entries were half-promised for the Italian Grand Prix, but whether from fear of another defeat by the P2 Alfas, or merely a question of expense, none of them materialized.

Yet at the San Sebastian Grand Prix in Spain a month before Monza the boot was on the other foot, for Sunbeam, Delage, Bugatti, Mercedes, Diatto and Schmid were all represented, and only Alfa Romeo were absent. Were the Italians a little unsure of their ability to win when the blown Sunbeams were running really well? The British cars were, in fact, in fine fettle, Segrave winning in masterly style from Costantini's Bugatti and two Delages; but Kenelm Lee Guinness's race, after beginning well, ended disastrously. Spanish labourers were instructed before the race to spread sand on some of the corners to diminish skidding, but found it easier to use clay dug from nearby fields. When it rained this made the course dangerously slippery, with the clay forming in ruts. Guinness's front wheels caught in these and the Sunbeam went into a wild slide, hit a bank and rolled over three times. It then hit a wall on the opposite side, Guinness and his mechanic Barratt being pitched out and plunging some 50 feet down a railway cutting. Barratt was killed instantly, while 'KLG' suffered head injuries which ended his brilliant racing career and affected his entire subsequent life.

The strain of racing for over 7 hours in August heat to cover 503 miles shows in the faces of the 1924 Grand Prix victors, Giuseppe Campari and his riding mechanic Attilio Marinoni. They won at 70.98 mph by over a minute from the twelve-cylinder Delages of Divo and Benoist, with Wagner fourth in another P2 Alfa, Segrave (Sunbeam), Thomas (Delage) and the two Bugattis of Chassagne and Friedrich.

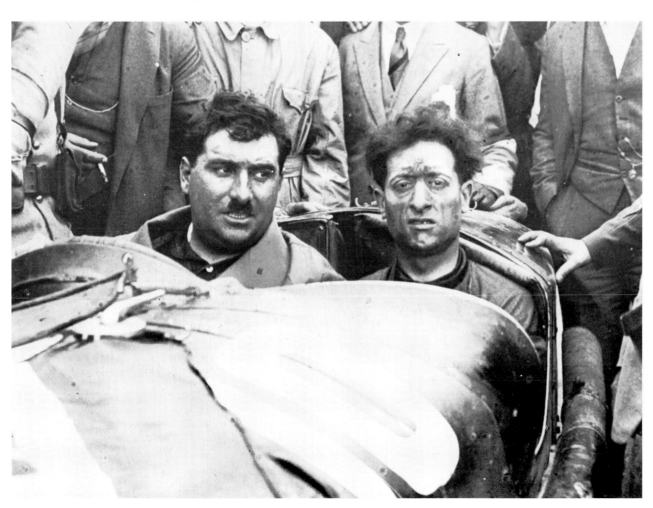

Other tragedies marred an otherwise brilliant season. Dario Resta, another famous Sunbeam driver, lost his life at Brooklands during a record attempt; a rear tyre was punctured, and the inner tube wrapped itself around the rear brake controls, locking the wheel up. The United States lost two great racing sons when Jimmy Murphy, 1921 Grand Prix and 1922 Indianapolis winner, and Joe Boyer, 1924 Indianapolis winner, were both killed in speedway accidents.

Two new circuits, at Montlhéry outside Paris, and Miramas, inland of Marseilles, were opened, but another course, Sitges in Spain, was to have a brief career, its high, steep bankings being deemed dangerous. The Talbot-Darracqs appeared in updated form with superchargers, and remained 'the Invincibles' by winning every 1924 race they contested. Their success included the first Swiss Grand Prix, run at Meyrin, near Geneva, and the fourth 200 Miles Race at Brooklands, these events marking K. Lee Guinness's last two victories.

Abroad, Enzo Ferrari, who was too unwell to drive in the French Grand Prix, atoned by winning three other races for Alfa Romeo—at Savio, Polesine and in the first Coppa Acerbo at Pescara. Tazio Nuvolari, second in a Chiribiri to Ferrari at

Polesine, won the first of countless car race wins at Tigullio, driving a Bianchi. Rudolf Caracciola scored his first race win for Mercedes in the Eifelrennen at Nideggen. On the so-called 'touring car' front, a very fine British victory was scored in the second Le Mans 24 Hours by John Duff and Frank Clement, driving the same 3-litre Bentley with which they placed fifth in 1923. It had been much improved with four-wheel brakes, but remained Duff's own private entry, facing forty French cars including works Lorraine, Chenard and Bignan teams.

This freak accident took place at the Culver City board track in the USA during the 250 miles race of 1924. Stuart Wilkinson tangled with another car, his 2-litre Miller shedding its front axle and hitting the top safety rail stern on. With 100 mph impetus the tail wedged itself firmly between rail and track, Wilkinson emerging practically unhurt.

Road racing, 1924: De Hane Segrave's winning supercharged six-cylinder Sunbeam coming through the narrow main street of Oria during the 1924 San Sebastian Grand Prix in Spain. The race was run in heavy drizzle over the 11.03-mile Lasarte circuit, where hazards included low walls, high walls, steep banks, tramlines, excessive camber, ditches, a narrow archway under Hernani town hall, and clay put down by indolent workmen instead of sand to stop skidding.

SABOTAGE ATTEMPT

That year the Le Mans rules required drivers to stop after five laps, erect their hoods, and complete two laps with them in position. The Bentley had its dramas, including a locked gear-change caused by a coachbuilder's staple jamming the gate, and a 'swollen hub' which prolonged a wheel change made 1½ hours before the finish. In truth it was a small grub screw, craftily inserted by someone anxious that the Bentley should not win, but fortunately discovered by Clement. The British car's winning margin of 10 miles over two Lorraines could thus have been greater.

Italy tried a 24-hour touring car race at Monza that year, the *Gran Premio della Notte* or 'Grand Prix of the Night', and to her surprise the home-based Alfa Romeo, Diatto and OM entries were all trounced by a German 2.6-litre NAG driven by Riecken and

Sombre scene at Aldeamuro, when Kenelm Lee Guinness's Sunbeam was deflected off course by deep ruts of clay, struck a wall, and plunged down a 50-ft railway embankment during the San Sebastian race. Barratt, the mechanic, was killed, while Guinness's injuries ended his brilliant racing career.

Berthold. An unaccustomed second were Ascari/Marinoni in an RL Alfa Romeo, while a Diatto was the first 2-litre finisher. Germany took racing successes seriously, and the victorious NAG drivers got a tremendous welcome from thousands of Berliners on their return from Italy. The four-cylinder sports NAG thereafter was naturally called the 'Monza', one of the better German sports cars of the time. In similar manner, a well-known French sports model, the 1100 cc Salmson, earned its name 'San Sebastian' by winning the 1924 Touring Grand Prix on that circuit in Northern Spain. Aided by a handicap formula and pouring rain, its driver, Oscar Leblanc, beat all the larger Bignan, Lorraine, Aries and Mercedes class winners.

Lastly, and as signs of the changing times, in order to save time the AC works driver J. A. Joyce and his mechanic flew by de Havilland aircraft from Croydon to Boulogne and back for speed trials there, and an aeroplane was used by Dunlop to fly special tyres out to the Bugatti team for the French Grand Prix at Lyons.

Post-race portrait: San Sebastian Grand Prix winner Segrave, in surprisingly clean white overalls, looks weary after six hours of racing and dispirited at the news of Guinness's crash. On the left is King Alfonso XIII of Spain, with Ettore Bugatti next to him, gesturing to the photographer; on the right, behind Segrave, are Divo, Morel, Louis Delage and Constantini (feeling for a match?) who made the fastest lap with his Type 35 Bugatti.

Pre-race conference: the Talbot-Darracq team talk things over before the 1924 200 Miles Race at Brooklands. Left to right: K. Lee Guinness, George Duller (back to camera), Segrave (in car), mechanic Hivernat, Parry Thomas (in Fair Isle jersey) and Capt. J. S. Irving. The cars scored another 1-2-3 success, Guinness winning at 102.27 mph.

The fourth and last year of the 2-litre Grand Prix Formula brought an important change. The AIACR decided that riding mechanics would no longer be carried in Grand Prix races, the driver relying instead on his own eyes to watch the instruments and a rear mirror. Although Segrave and Divo favoured his retention the general consensus of opinion was that the present 2-litre supercharged cars were fast and dangerous enough as it was, and that riding mechanics had a miserable time, got none of the glory, were of limited use, and were in needless danger of being killed.

Another interesting development was the establishment of a World Championship—not for drivers, as it is today, but for the manufacturers of the most successful car in four 1925 qualifying races, namely Indianapolis and the Belgian, French and Italian Grands Prix. At Indianapolis Peter de Paolo, nephew of the great Ralph de Palma, and his former riding mechanic, won in a supercharged Duesenberg from a new front-drive Miller at a record 101.13 mph. This was the first time that the 100 mph barrier had been broken at the speedway.

European interest there focused on Pietro Bordino, who after

Besides Brooklands, Sitges, Montlhéry and many US speedways, Germany could also boast a banked track in the 1920s—the Opel-Bahn at Russelsheim. This was actually the test track for Opel's main car factory, but race meetings were promoted there, with a natural bias towards Opel products. Here two rare Opel single-seaters put on a show, Fritz von Opel of the automobile factory leading the veteran driver Carl Joerns in a match race.

Treating them rough: the granite-paved and potholed Pont-à-Marq circuit saw a deserved 1-2 class success for the Italian Lancia Lambda with independent front suspension and unitary chassis/body construction in the annual 'Bad Roads Race' of 1924. Riva, winner of the 2- to 2.5-litre class, leads a La Licorne in the annual suspension-bashing, chassis-breaking contest, which was won outright by a 3-litre Chenard-Walcker with lath-and-canvas bodywork.

Fiat's withdrawal from the Grand Prix front had taken one of the 1924 2-litre cars across the Atlantic for a number of Californian speedway events. He had the car fitted with an American-built single-seater body, and won a 25-mile race at Culver City at a respectable 133.1 mph, and a 50-miler at Cotati. Then he took his *monoposto* Fiat to Indianapolis, finding the home-based centrifugally-blown Millers and Duesenbergs much faster then his Roots-blown car. According to de Paolo, 'frequent outbursts of unpleasant Italian cuss words could be heard from within the Bordino garage' when the Fiat was being prepared. Plug trouble early in the race was no help, and then at around the 200-mile mark the Italian hurt his hand and had to go for hospital treatment, while Mourre took over the Fiat. Bordino resumed driving later and finished the race in tenth place; clearly Indianapolis was becoming an American fortress which the Europeans could no longer storm.

Round 2 of the new Championship (which aroused singularly little interest) was the Belgian Grand Prix, shedding its former touring car character and donning the extra title for 1925 of 'the Grand Prix of Europe', for what that was worth. Run over 500 miles of the difficult Spa-Francorchamps circuit, it proved a disappointing race. Sunbeam entered and then withdrew, and Guyot did likewise, leaving four V12 Delages and three P2 Alfa

Racing reaches Switzerland: K. Lee Guinness in the 1500 cc supercharged twin ohc Talbot-Darracq takes the lead from Lepori's Fiat in the Swiss Voiturette Grand Prix of 1924. Behind is a Bignan, a Brescia Bugatti and Dario Resta in the other Talbot. The race was run on the Meyrin road course outside Geneva, and provided the Talbots with another runaway win, Guinness ahead of Resta, with Lepori's Fiat third.

Romeos to settle the issue. The Delages were now supercharged, but the installation was defective and the blue cars were easily outpaced by the red Alfas.

So large did the gap grow between the rival marques that Jano brought his drivers in for leisurely refreshment while the cars stood silent at the pits. After this insolent demonstration of their superiority, Ascari and Campari resumed the race, being the sole finishers following the retirement of their team-mate Brilli-Peri with a broken spring, and the entire Delage quartet. One gathers that M. Louis Delage was not pleased.

The invincible Talbot-Darracq voiturettes continued their 1-2-3 monopoly in the Grand Prix de l'Ouverture, held at the close of the 1924 season on the new Montlhéry banked speedway outside Paris. After each driver had a turn at leading, the 186.4-mile race was won by Jack E. Scales, with Segrave a length behind and Bourlier 15 yards further back. Segrave's fastest lap was at an impressive 109.6 mph.

Fêting the victors: when a German car won an International motor race in the barren early 1920s, Germany celebrated. In 1924 Riecken and Berthold, drivers of a 2.6-litre NAG, get a big reception in Berlin after winning Italy's first 24 hours touring car race, the Gran Premio della Notte *(Grand Prix of the Night) at Monza. In an outstanding drive the two Germans defeated the factory 3-litre Alfa Romeo of Ascari/Marinoni by 77 miles, with Italian Diatto and OM cars third and fourth.*

Then came the French Grand Prix, this time at Montlhéry on the new combined road and track, 7.8 miles per lap and hard on brakes. Despite its proclaimed nearness to Paris, which was supposed to bring vast crowds, eventually some 25,000 spectators turned up. They witnessed a long, dreary race with 621 miles to be covered, rain and a bad accident marring the day. Alfa Romeo, Delage, Sunbeam and Bugatti entries totalled fourteen, and for the first time in a French Grand Prix the ACF had to swallow their pride and offer substantial prize money — 150,000, 30,000 and 20,000 francs respectively for first, second and third home.

Montlhéry's *circuit routier* was very new, and as at Lyons in 1924 the French delineated many of the corners quickly and cheaply with wooden paling fences. From the start Antonio Ascari (who had voiced his disapproval of the fencing) blasted into the lead as usual, and by quarter-distance the meteoric Italian had 3½ minutes on the second car. Then it began to drizzle, and when the P2 hit a wet patch on a fast left-hand bend it slid, a hubcap catching in the paling fence. The car tore down over 100 yards of the fencing, then overturned in a ditch, Ascari being killed.

This tragedy caused the withdrawal of the remaining Alfas, and Delage inherited the race. Robert Benoist, erstwhile Salmson driver, was the victor, followed by Wagner in another Delage, Count Giulio Masetti taking third place for Sunbeam in their last French Grand Prix, while the next five cars were unblown Bugattis. After a melancholy fêting of the winners, Benoist and Masetti as representatives of Delage and Sunbeam laid their bouquets where Ascari had crashed; a sad conclusion to the first French victory in her own Grand Prix since 1913.

Alfa Romeo and Delage were now equal in the Championship, with Duesenberg 1 point behind, and the Italian Grand Prix was the decider. Delage spoiled interest in the contest by deciding not to go to Monza, but two Duesenbergs came over from the States, driven by one-eyed Tommy Milton and Pete Kreis. These were track-type single-seaters, and to comply with European minimum width rules their cockpits had to be widened with grotesque bulges. The blue-and-white cars with their centrifugally-blown 2-litre straight-eight engines screamed down the Monza straights at high speed, but track-type brakes and transmission served them less well on the corners.

Even so, the 'Dueseys' greatly enlivened the race. Kreis took the lead from Campari on lap 2 to a roar from the stands, only to

Try-out: for the 1924 Grand Prix season Sunbeam of Wolverhampton supercharged their 1923-type 2-litre six-cylinder engine and fitted it in a modified, longer wheelbase chassis. Dario Resta (former Indianapolis 500 Miles and American Grand Prix winner with Peugeot cars) took the new Sunbeam to two British hillclimbs at Aston Clinton and South Harting in May, and won both. Here Resta and the car pose at South Harting, with J. S. Irving, who was responsible for the supercharging, holding up the scoreboard.

Fiat's ace driver Pietro Bordino took a supercharged 1924 GP type car out to the United States for some track races including the 1925 Indianapolis 500 Miles. Single-seater bodywork was fitted in California, and Bordino won races at Culver City and Cotati, and finished tenth at Indianapolis. The road racing four-wheel brakes were retained, but the monoposto body, rear wheel discs and large diameter low-pressure tyres give the Fiat a strange appearance.

spin wildly at Lesmo, where excited spectators helped him back into the race — and that meant disqualification. Meanwhile Milton's car had a broken front damper and its gearbox stuck in top gear, but he caught his compatriot Peter de Paolo, driving one of the P2 Alfa Romeos. When the other two Italian cars stopped for fuel and tyres the Duesenberg shot ahead; the stands buzzed and Milton led for seven rounds until a very slow pit stop and a broken oil pipe set him right back.

Eventually Milton worked back to fourth place behind winner Brilli-Peri, Campari and Costantini (Bugatti), who won the 1500 cc class. De Paolo in the third Alfa was fifth after carburettor troubles, followed by three more Bugattis. A new eight-cylinder Diatto designed by Alfieri Maserati had taken part driven by E. Materassi, but was completed so late that one hasty coat of red paint on the aluminium body gave it a pink hue. It retired early, as did a Guyot, a British Eldridge Special with Anzani engine, and two Chiribiris, one of which rolled four times on a turn, ending up neatly on its wheels with the driver completely unhurt.

So Alfa Romeo emerged as the first World Champions. The Delage team, having avoided confrontation with them, managed to get to San Sebastian for the Grand Prix of Spain a fortnight later, whereas Alfas had not entered. Britain was represented by a single Sunbeam driven by Masetti and the Eldridge Special, while five Bugattis also ran. The Delage quartet showed themselves faster than the ageing Sunbeam, in which Masetti lay fourth with the Delage No. 4 driver, Torchy, chasing him. In his efforts to get by, unfortunately, Torchy lost control at a corner, crashed and was killed. The Sunbeam dropped out at half-distance, and the remaining Delages of Divo, Benoist and Thomas came home in formation, trailed by four Bugattis.

Belgian walkover: Antonio Ascari makes a pit stop during the 1925 Grand Prix of Europe at Spa-Francorchamps in Belgium. The offside front tyre is badly worn and the front axle is up on the jack for a wheel-change, but Ascari's lead was so great that he could afford a comparatively leisurely stop, with only one mechanic to help him. He won the 500 mile race by 22 minutes from his team-mate Campari, the two P2 Alfa Romeos being the only cars to finish.

BUGATTIS SHINE

In non-Championship events abroad, Ettore Bugatti's lovely Type 35, the first Grand Prix car to be sold to private exponents, was appearing in the hands of wealthy amateurs. Count Carlo Masetti, brother of the Sunbeam and Talbot driver, won the first Rome Grand Prix with one; Count Maggi won the Circuit of Garda, while in the Grand Prix de Provence at Miramas Vidal pipped Glen Kidston to the post. Kidston brought his Type 35 to Brooklands for the Easter meeting, giving English enthusiasts their first sight of a classic-to-be.

It performed well, winning one race at 96.84 mph and placing third in another, despite the ugly silencer disfiguring its nearside. The iniquitous Brooklands silencer had, in fact, become obligatory the previous year, thanks to clamorous and hypersensitive local residents being able to inflict this imposition despite the fact that their houses were built long after the track was opened. No other circuit anywhere in the world required the

The 2-litre racing Duesenberg and its 'counterpart' 4¼-litre Model A touring car of the mid-1920s. Although both had straight-eight engines and shared some axle, steering and other components, there was very little real similarity despite Duesenberg publicity efforts to convince their clientele. The racing cars, winners of the Indianapolis '500' in 1924 and 1925 and numerous other American races, had twin ohc, centrifugally supercharged engines of 122 cu.in. (2 litres) capacity, small narrow chassis and single-seater bodies.

fitting of silencers, a handicap which affected racing at Brooklands up to its demise in 1939.

Voiturette racing saw the unbeaten Talbots in their fifth season, running this time as 'Darracqs' by some mysterious STD whim, and taking the honours at Miramas, Montlhéry and in the JCC 200 Miles. For the first time at Brooklands an attempt at simulating road race conditions was made by installing artificial corners where the public could see and hear the cars braking, changing down, cornering and accelerating. Thus 'the largest crowd ever seen at Brooklands' (*vide The Light Car,* but perhaps 30,000) gathered thickly and watched Segrave and Masetti take a stage-managed 1-2 for Darracq with masterly ease, although team-mate Conelli retired on lap 1.

With typical British conservatism, riding mechanics were carried, although the AIACR had decided that they could be dispensed with in Grand Prix cars. More sensible in Britain was the growing habit of wearing crash helmets, pioneered by Segrave and S. C. H. Davis. A running commentary on the '200' was given over '2LO' on the wireless, while special trains were laid on by the Southern Railway; the fast return to Waterloo was mis-scheduled to leave before the race had finished—SR could slip up long before BR!

Refreshments for man and motor: Albert Divo, lying third in the 1925 Grand Prix of Europe at Spa, Belgium, applies himself to the bottle while his Delage is refuelled. Four of the French V12s were entered in revised form with twin superchargers and 5-speed gearboxes, but they performed poorly owing to supercharging defects, and all retired. Ascari, the unchallenged victor, storms past the halted Delage.

At the Virage du Gendarme: Robert Benoist (twelve-cylinder Delage) cuts in close to the paling fence at one of the S-bends on the new Montlhéry road circuit, completed in time for the 1925 French Grand Prix. The organizers' addiction to this kind of fencing resulted in the death of race leader Ascari, Benoist and Divo sharing victory for Delage following the withdrawal of the Alfa Romeo team.

Artist at work: Italian-born Bartolomeo Constantini cornering at Montlhéry during the 1925 French Grand Prix. Headed only by supercharged cars, he finished fourth, leading a quintet of unblown 2-litre Type 35 Bugattis which showed impressive reliability and regularity in the over-long 621-mile race. Note the absence of a riding mechanic, dispensed with from 1925 on in the interests of safety.

A much more genuine, and alarming, finish took place at Montlhéry in the second Grand Prix de l'Ouverture. Finishing orders in the Talbot team were generally decided before the race, either by tossing a coin or by Coatalen decree, but perhaps they were left open at Montlhéry. At any rate, on the last lap and on slippery wet concrete, the Italian Count Conelli, normally a calm, heady driver, suddenly pulled out in a bid to snatch the lead from team-mate George Duller as they tore up to the finishing line. Conelli's car skidded, struck a barrier, spun three times, then overturned, ploughed along on its scuttle for a dozen yards or so, then slewed, rolled again, and ended up on its wheels, throwing a stunned Conelli out. Amazingly he revived quickly and walked to the first aid station, and the car, scarcely damaged, was driven back to the works an hour later!

Turning to sports car racing, Le Mans was now a calendar 'regular', and the British looked eagerly to Bentleys for another good performance. They were disappointed this time, for, although Bentley sent a works 3-litre in support of Duff's private entry, both retired with fuel trouble. Instead a 3-litre six-cylinder twin ohc Sunbeam driven by S. C. H. ('Sammy') Davis and Jean Chassagne upheld 'the green', finishing second to a 3½-litre Lorraine-Dietrich. A new 24 Hours race was that of Belgium, held at Spa, where the Lorraines had to give best to a Chenard-Walcker, while driver/manufacturer Robert Sénéchal drove his 750 cc Sénéchal the entire 24 hours without relief in true Bol d'Or style.

As a result of objections against noise from local residents, the Brooklands authorities agreed to make silencers compulsory from 1924 on. Mechanically these unwelcome fittings caused undue back pressure and inhibited performance, while the aesthetic effect of the ugly exhaust boxes can be seen on this private Type 35 Bugatti, purchased in 1925 by the wealthy and talented amateur Glen Kidston.

There was a marked revival of racing in Germany. Although German entries were accepted by Italy and the USA, the French remained adamant and no German cars or drivers could yet run in their precious Grand Prix. The Germans retaliated by excluding foreign cars from their motor shows and foreign drivers from their races, which were pretty minor anyway. In 1925, however, the AIACR voted 12 to 2, with 4 abstentions, to re-admit Germany as a member, whereupon the Automobil Club von Deutschland announced a new race, the Hindenburg Cup, to be run over the old Taunus circuit used in 1904 for the fifth Gordon Bennett race and in 1907 for the Kaiserpreis.

British innovation: the enterprising Alvis company began experimenting with front-wheel-drive cars in 1925, and ran two in that year's 200 Mile Race at Brooklands. This is C. M. Harvey taking an over-generous swing through one of the artificial 'sandbank' corners; he was still running when the race ended, fifth among the 1½-litre cars.

Count Giulio Masetti in No. 5 Sunbeam goes hard after Albert Divo's Delage at the start of the 1925 Grand Prix of Spain at San Sebastian. In the famous British marque's last appearance in a classic race, Masetti retired after 22 laps.

The French predilection for
bizarre streamlining did not
prevent the famous little 1100 cc
Chenard-Walcker 'Tank' from
scoring numerous touring and
sports car successes. Lagache,
here, has just won the 325-mile
Georges Boillot Cup race at
Boulogne in 1925. The
four-cylinder engine had pushrod
ohv with auxiliary rotary exhaust
valves; the bodywork was made
in duralumin, the rear wheels
being enclosed. A 'Tank'
Chenard won the 24 Hours Bol
d'Or race at late as 1937.

An interesting aspect of the
23½-mile Boulogne road circuit,
with Boris Ivanowski's 1100 cc
SCAP-engined BNC coming up
the hill during the 1925
Boulogne race for light cars
and voiturettes. The car finished
fourth in the voiturette class
behind a Brescia Bugatti and
two Sénéchals. Those flimsy
wooden barriers edging the
pavement would not do in the
1980s!

'Hoods up' was the order for the
first 20 laps (215 miles) of the
1925 Le Mans 24 Hours race,
causing the undoing of H.
(Bertie) Kensington Moir's works
3-litre Bentley from Britain. The
extra wind resistance of the hood,
coupled with some over-eager
duelling with Segrave's 3-litre
Sunbeam, saw the Bentley dry of
fuel and stranded out on the
circuit half a lap before Moir's
scheduled refuel stop.

Above: on the final lap of the 1925 Grand Prix de l'Ouverture at Montlhéry, Count Conelli's Talbot skidded on the wet concrete, hit the wall, spun twice, rolled over as it crossed the line, then righted itself again, the driver very luckily being hurt only superficially about the head.

Centre: the futuristic 2-litre rear-engined Grand Prix Benz scored an unexpected success at the opening meeting of the Solitude circuit near Stuttgart in May 1925. Driving the Tropfenwagen (Teardrop-car) Franz Horner won the main event on the 8.55-mile circuit, lapping at 56.5 mph.

Left: typifying the aero-engined monsters that were raced at Brooklands track in early post-war years was this Isotta-Maybach with 20½-litre Maybach six-cylinder aero-engine in a 1907 chain-driven Isotta-Fraschini chassis, built by E. A. D. Eldridge. Driving this car at the 1924 Easter meeting, Le Champion won the Founders' Gold Cup race at 104.25 mph, turning one lap at 114.75 mph.

69

Fiat v. Leyland: in July 1925 a memorable 3-lap match race took place at Brooklands between Ernest Eldridge driving his Fiat 'Mephistopheles' (above) and J. G. Parry Thomas with his 7.3-litre straight-eight Leyland-Thomas (right) which held the Outer Circuit lap record. Eldridge's machine had a 21.7-litre six-cylinder Fiat aero-engine in a lengthened 1907 Fiat chassis, and had broken the World Land Speed Record in 1924 at 146.01 mph, but it could not hold off Thomas's Leyland. After a dramatic struggle, during which both cars threw tyre treads, Thomas took the lead on the last lap to win at 123.23 mph with a fastest lap at 129.70 mph.

A CURIOUS RACE

The race was International with qualifications, foreign entrants having to belong to a club or organization on friendly terms with the AvD! Two Frenchmen, P. Clause and M. Colvill, went with a pair of 2-litre Bignans, Lams of Belgium drove a Mathis, and the Czech Morawitz brought along a Bugatti, but most entries were German. Disappointingly the Mercedes, NAG and Benz firms decided not to compete officially, but NSU ran four small six-cylinder cars with superchargers, unusually driven off the gearbox with very long intake manifolds. Adolf Rosenberger lay

well up with a blown 1½-litre Mercedes, making fastest lap before retiring, and the Cup was won by 20 year-old August Momberger (who later drove in the Auto Union Grand Prix team) who outpaced all the larger cars in his 1.3-litre NSU.

A similar NSU was second, a Bugatti won the 2-litre class from Clause (Bignan), while Deilman with a NAG 'Monza' took the 2.6-litre class. Over-all the Hindenburg Cup, which some German historians regard as the first German Grand Prix, proved a dull race on poor roads, and it was not repeated. More successful was the opening meeting at the new 8.55-mile Solitude circuit, set in woods outside Stuttgart, where a claimed 300,000 spectators swarmed to watch the racing. Christian Werner opened the course in a blown Mercedes, and races for three classes were run off. One of the ultra-modern rear-engined Benz *Tropfenwagen* proved fastest of the day, beating a Bugatti and a big Stoewer and prompting speculation on 'what might have been'.

Mit kompressor: a successful German sports-racing car built in 1.3- and 1.5-litre forms was the six-cylinder side-valve NSU, with Roots-type supercharger driven off the 4-speed gearbox. With 20-year-old August Momberger at the wheel, one of these NSUs won the 270-mile Hindenburg Cup race, held in 1925 over the old Kaiserpreis circuit of 1907. Others won at Avus, Solitude and in numerous hillclimbs.

Britain's premier hillclimb, Shelsley Walsh in Worcestershire, gave promise in 1925 of a keen struggle between the specialist Raymond Mays (top picture) driving a new, supercharged 1½-litre single-seater AC, and the all-rounder H. O. D. Segrave (centre) with the 2-litre supercharged Grand Prix Sunbeam. Alas, the AC suffered dire ignition trouble and did not even 'place', whereas Segrave scored a most polished FTD in the rain.

Another prominent performer at Shelsley Walsh, and also in Southport sand races and other northern events, was Miss May Cunliffe, seen here climbing the famous Worcestershire 1000 yards hill in her 3-litre Bentley, one of the 1922 TT cars, still with its flat radiator.

Gallic vintage: d'Aulau's 2.4-litre four-cylinder Hotchkiss sweeps through one of the 17 turns in Les 17 Tournants *hillclimb of 1925. A solid, reliable, lively tourer, it broke no records but scored a class 'third'.*

Had Benz had the resources for further development of this remarkable car, perhaps by supercharging and improving the suspension, Grand Prix design could well have made a spectacular advance. As it was, Benz and Mercedes were both feeling the economic pinch severely, and were in the throes of negotiation to form a merger with the prior aim of ensuring their respective survivals. When the new Mercedes-Benz company came into being the following year, some exciting future racing cars were assured, but the prophetic *Tropfenwagen*, alas, was not among them.

A sad tailpiece to Britain's own domestic 'golden age' of sprints and hillclimbs came in 1925, when the breaking of a spectator's leg ended legal tolerance of the holding of such events on public roads. The fateful incident took place at Kop hill, Essex, early in the season, when F. Giveen's Brescia Bugatti slid wide at a corner, mounted a bank and struck the spectator. The latter was in an area forbidden by the organizers, but had insisted on exercising his right as a member of the public to remain there. The RAC announced that no further permits for speed contests on the public highway would be granted, and the folly of an unthinking minority of the public thus deprived British enthusiasts of a unique spectacle. Future sprints and hillclimbs were confined to courses on private land, such as the famous Shelsley Walsh hill, on promenades such as Madeira Drive, Brighton, and on beaches.

* * *

4
FADING GLORIES
1926-27

Although the modern 3-litre Grand Prix Formula 1 has broken all records for longevity, the average life of earlier racing Formulae was much shorter. Over half a century ago, four years was thought long enough for the 2-litre rules of the 1922–25 'Golden Age'. Early in 1925 the AIACR already gave hints that for 1926–27 Grands Prix engine size would be cut to 1½ litres, with or without superchargers, bodies would require only one seat, and minimum weight would be down to 550 kg (1212 lb). This precipitated a great fuss to the effect that such cars would be too light and too fast for even the finest drivers to cope with; so the AIACR had a rethink, and in July their Sporting Commission (CSI) announced that in fact bodies with two seats and 31 inches wide, as used in 1925, would be retained, although no mechanic would occupy the second seat, while the proposed minimum weight was raised to 700 kg (1543 lb).

Opposite: in 1926 Delage produced a new twin-supercharged 1½-litre straight-eight, but in its first race, the Grand Prix of Europe at San Sebastian in Spain, the cars ran so hot that the drivers wilted from the heat. Robert Sénéchal was hastily recruited as a 'stand-in' for Bourlier's No. 15.

Below: the 'pilot' Hispano-Suiza pulls to one side, and Benoist in one of the new Delages leads the Grand Prix of Europe, followed by Goux and Costantini in Bugattis.

Putting on a show; despite complete lack of opposition, and his two Bugatti team-mates out of the running, Jules Goux tries hard to entertain the sparse crowd at Miramas while winning the 1926 French Grand Prix, a fiasco of a race with but three starters and two finishers.

These rules seemed more acceptable, prompting blithe talk of several teams of cars. Reality was more dampening, however. Manufacturers were feeling the mid-20s pinch somewhat, and, with expensive supercharged high-revving multi-cylinder engines a *sine qua non* for racing success, contenders were few. Sunbeam had gone, although new Talbot-Darracqs from the same STD group were promised. Alfa Romeo had gone, selling two of their P2s to Italians and two to Swiss amateurs. Delage, however, were working on new cars, while Ettore Bugatti had his existing '1500s', requiring only superchargers to become competitive. There were more shadowy promises of strange two-strokes from Fiat and Sima-Violet, an OM team from Italy, of front-drive Alvises, and Thomas, Eldridge and Halford Specials from Britain. Had all these cars materialized, how excellent a season would 1926 have been. As it was. . . .

The first race under the new 1500 cc rules, and the first European round in the second so-called World Championship, was the French Grand Prix, held in late June at Miramas, near Marseilles. This uninteresting oval, master-minded by former racing driver Paul Bablot and the AC de Marseille, was laid in a desert area called Sulauze, covered with myriads of small stones seemingly ideal to make concrete for the track. Unfortunately,

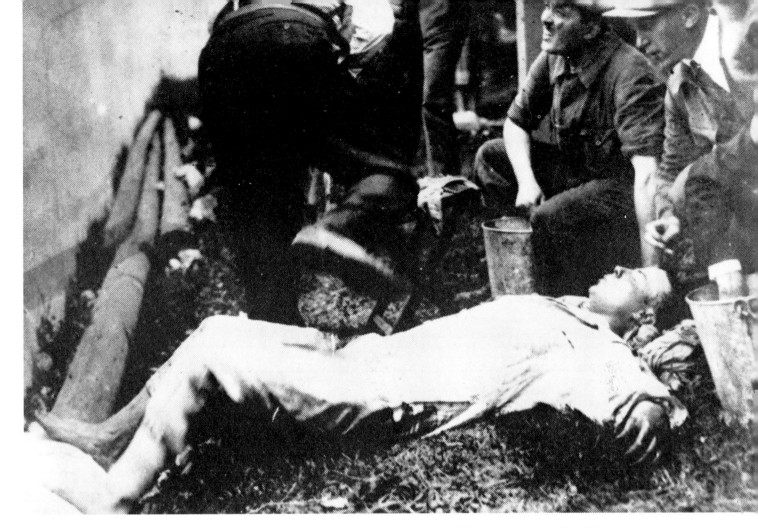

as the cement set it settled, leaving the stones standing some-what proud, and giving a rough surface very hard on tyres.

The track, 5 kilometres (3.1 miles) round, was simply a lozenge-shaped oblong with wide, slightly banked turns at each end, but two tight loops were inserted in the straights for the Grand Prix to add interest. An enormous cantilever-roofed grandstand was built in concrete, and all it required to be filled was a good entry. Alas for Bablot and the AC de Marseille: Delage, Talbot, Sima-Violet and Bugatti entries had been received, but the first three marques were unready, and all scratched, leaving just three blown straight-eight Bugattis to contest the great French Grand Prix!

Race day was hot, and not surprisingly spectators were few, especially with the railway station a 6 km walk, or a stuffy bus ride, from the circuit. From the start Pierre de Viscaya set the pace until supercharger trouble forced him out just before half-distance. 'Meo' Costantini's car was similarly afflicted and lost many laps, whereas Jules Goux drove as if in combat with five rival teams, providing the only real entertainment for the sparse crowd. He won the 311-mile 'race' at 68.16 mph, with Costantini flagged off 15 laps in arrears; it was the worst fiasco in racing history.

Heat exhaustion hits Delage driver Edmond Bourlier, who has to be revived in the shade behind the San Sebastian pits in the early stages of the Grand Prix of Europe; note the blisters on his throttle foot. The exhaust systems on the 1926 Delages passed too close to the cockpits on the drivers' side, heating the pedals and in some cases burning through the light alloy body sides.

The next Championship round was at San Sebastian, Spain, and after the Miramas débâcle the organizers spent anxious days wondering which of the twenty-one entries received would actually turn up. Talbot and Sima-Violet again promised, only to defect, and OM, Guyot, Jean Gras and Eldridge did likewise, but this time Delage's new cars were ready to run against a Bugatti trio. Hot sunshine, a scorching *sirocco* wind, and flying dust clouds made the prospect of 484 racing miles grim for drivers. A rolling start was arranged, the six cars being headed by a big touring Hispano-Suiza containing a high official with a flag to release the pack. Unfortunately 'the car of kings' chose so public a moment to have starter trouble, and had to be pushstarted.

The Delages — superb low-built blown straight-eights — showed superior speed, but as the laps unreeled their drivers began to wilt under the heat, not only from the Spanish sun but also from their own engines and exhaust pipes running uncomfortably close to the cockpit sides. André Morel pulled in on lap 11, collapsed, and was whisked to hospital with sunstroke and burnt feet, while veteran Louis Wagner (who raced Darracqs in 1903!) took over. Three laps later Benoist came in, tottered against the pit, then dropped. Medical attendants rushed, and Réné Thomas, reserve driver, reluctantly prepared himself for the ordeal of driving a 'travelling oven'.

Britain gets a Grand Prix: start of the first British Grand Prix, held at Brooklands on 7 August, 1926. Segrave and Divo (Talbots) and Sénéchal (Delage) have beaten the camera, followed here by Campbell (Bugatti No. 7), Eyston (Aston Martin 3), Moriceau (Talbot 6), Benoist (Delage 2), Halford (Halford Special 5) and Wagner (Delage 14)—the eventual winner.

SÉNÉCHAL VOLUNTEERS

Then up rushed the eager Robert Sénéchal, Bol d'Or 24 hours endurance specialist, and volunteered to drive the car. Thomas looked hopefully at Louis Delage; 'D'accord', assented the patron, and off went Sénéchal. Then Wagner returned for foot treatment, as did Sénéchal after six valiant laps, the two Delages standing silent at the pits, while a mechanic tried to cut cooling holes in them. In the meantime the Bugattis were well ahead, when suddenly the wind changed, bringing a delicious coolness and bringing the Delage drivers back to life. Benoist and Wagner set off with a will, both breaking the lap record in their pursuit of the 'Bugs', while Sénéchal drove a second spell too. It was too late, however, to catch Goux, who won a grilling race at 70.5 mph, with the Bourlier/Morel/Sénéchal Delage second, and another Bugatti third. The other Delages placed fourth and sixth, but the race officials decided to disqualify the two driven by Sénéchal as he had not been nominated beforehand. Louis Delage protested at this Spanish bureaucracy, but three months elapsed before the cars were reinstated.

By then their drivers had endured a second cooking in the first British Grand Prix ever to be held. Brooklands track in Surrey was the venue, and the race took place in August, by which time the eagerly awaited Grand Prix Talbots were ready. These had supercharged straight-eight engines in chassis as low as the

Anglo-French: wearing British racing green, but built in France, the two new eight-cylinder Talbots of Segrave and Divo showed their pace early in the race by leading the Delages. Segrave made the fastest lap at 85.99 mph, but the cars lacked stamina, both retiring.

Delages but even more comely with inclined radiators and pointed tails. Unfortunately Bugatti decided not to send a team, but Malcolm Campbell entered an ex-works car which he had just acquired, having time to replace the alloy wheels with Rudge type hubs and wire wheels before race day.

Only G. E. T. Eyston (Anzani-engined Aston Martin special) and F. B. Halford (Halford Special) started of six British entries, but surprisingly the three Talbots, though built at Suresnes, Paris, were nominated as 'British' and painted in British green! The circuit followed 1925 200 Miles style, with artificial S-bends closely overlooked by the crowd. Their first thrill came soon after the start, when the tubular front axle of Moriceau's Talbot broke in the middle under braking at the first turn on the first lap. The other Talbots came through fast, but were erratic in performance, although Segrave tried very hard and made fastest lap before retiring with diverse troubles.

Benoist's Delage led the race until a joint in its exhaust system broke, allowing scorching hot gases to play on the cockpit sides and pedals. Wagner's Delage developed similar symptoms, the escaping heat burning a hole in the body, whereupon he stopped at the pits and plunged his feet into a pan of cold water. A dejected Benoist followed suit, and when Wagner set off again his car began misfiring so badly that it had to be retired. After a second paddle he took over Sénéchal's leading car, while Benoist's engine next caught fire, extinguishers going into action with Gallic zest. A few laps later it happened again, and a very fed-up driver handed over to Dubonnet and made painfully for a pan of water to douse his scorched feet.

Benoist's trouble allowed Malcolm Campbell, driving one of his best races ever, into second place with the wire-wheeled Bugatti, while, apart from yet another footbath by Wagner, he and Sénéchal eventually won, both drivers looking distinctly 'second-hand'. As a change from the childish modern habit of the race victor spraying champagne over all and sundry, Wagner had his poured over his head. . . .

ENTER MASERATI

The fifth and final Championship round, the Italian/European Grand Prix at Monza, reverted to near-Miramas standards, with but two Maseratis — a new marque from Bologna — and an aged Chiribiri to offset a Bugatti trio. Sadly neither Talbot nor Delage went to make a real race of it, while three new Brescia-built blown straight-eight OMs were withdrawn. With more imagination than those at Miramas, the organizers therefore merged the *Gran Premio* with the 1100 cc supporting race, thus giving at least the illusion of a good entry at the massed start.

The Maseratis were practical-looking cars with the fashionable Roots-blown straight-eight power units, obviously derived from

An impressive view of the new Amilcar 1100 cc six-cylinder Type C6 racing voiturette, with twin overhead camshafts, large Roots-type supercharger, and oil tank carried between the front dumbirons. These beautiful little cars dominated their class for several years, and were still winning races a decade later.

Above: three of the new Bologna-built straight-eight supercharged Maserati racing cars being prepared for the classic Targa Florio in Sicily. On their first appearance, in the 1926 race, Alfieri Maserati won the 1½-litre class.

Left: the French driver 'Sabipa' unexpectedly won the 1926 Italian Grand Prix at Monza in a Bugatti after Meo Costantini's works car seized its engine when holding a 25-mile lead with only 2½ laps to go.

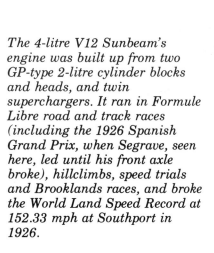

Officine Meccaniche of Brescia built the OM, a sturdy medium-sized car with a side-valve six-cylinder engine. The picture shows the works-supported semi-amateur Renato Balestrero driving in the 1926 Targa Florio, in which he finished eighth. He won the Messina Cup race both in 1925 and 1926, and the first Tripoli Grand Prix in 1925, while an OM works team finished first, second and third in the first Mille Miglia sports car race in 1927.

the Maserati-designed 2-litre Diatto of 1925. One had placed first in the 1½-litre class of the 1926 Targa Florio early in the season, so a measure of raceworthiness could be expected. Designer/driver Alfieri Maserati and Emilio Materassi certainly did their best at Monza, hanging on to Costantini's leading Bugatti from the start, and holding off Goux and 'Sabipa'. Alas, experimental supercharger drives let the Maseratis down, and both cars were out after six laps.

With them went much of the interest, although Serboli's Chiribiri created alarm by catching fire at speed. The flames crept forward from the tail, forcing the driver to stand up in the cockpit; frantically applying the handbrake, he waited agonizing

The 4-litre V12 Sunbeam's engine was built up from two GP-type 2-litre cylinder blocks and heads, and twin superchargers. It ran in Formule Libre road and track races (including the 1926 Spanish Grand Prix, when Segrave, seen here, led until his front axle broke), hillclimbs, speed trials and Brooklands races, and broke the World Land Speed Record at 152.33 mph at Southport in 1926.

seconds while the speed dropped before jumping out, the car running on into the pit area where urgent hands stopped it. Firemen put out the blaze, while a thoughtful mechanic threw a bucket of water over Serboli's own overheated stern!

Goux's Bugatti broke an oil pump, but the brilliant Bartolomeo Costantini in the sister car held a commanding lead until just 2½ laps from the finish of the 60-lap, 372-mile race. Then his engine seized. Twenty-five miles behind came another Bugatti driven by 'Sabipa', a French amateur whose real name was Charavel, and as they sweated on Costantini's engine at the pits 'Sabipa' steadily closed the gap and passed into the lead. A bitter moment it must have been for Costantini after leading from the start and thrice breaking the lap record. Eventually he got going again, his Bugatti very sick, to stammer home second.

Thus Bugatti easily won the second World Championship, with three wins to one each by Delage and Miller, the latter at Indianapolis. The contest cannot be said to have inflamed the motor racing world in the exaggerated way its modern equivalent does. Indeed, an often more exciting by-product of the 1½-litre rules was the *Formule Libre* (Free Formula) class wherein organizers could promote races free of capacity restrictions, and manufacturers or owners could exercise obsolete or oversize cars. In this 'rebel group' four 1926 races proved outstanding.

Out for the Count: the end of Count Aymo Maggi's 1927 Targa Florio came very definitely on lap 5, when his 1½-litre eight-cylinder supercharged Maserati broke its chassis on the unforgiving Madonie circuit.

Grosser Preis von Deutschland: *Germany's first Grand Prix took place in 1926 on the 12¼-mile Avus track in the Grunewald district of Berlin. Lining up to take their places on the starting grid are the NSU works team, on the left, with an Austro-Daimler (No. 4) and an NAG (No. 5) coming by.*

The Rome Grand Prix, over a 5-mile road course outside 'the Eternal City', drew eighteen starters, including Masetti's 2-litre Sunbeam, two P2 Alfa Romeos and several Bugattis, one of which, a 2-litre driven by Count Maggi, defeated the P2s in fair fight. That Rome race was the great Giulio Masetti's last. In the Targa Florio a month later — ironically his favourite race — he drove one of four 2-litre V12 Delages (the redundant 1925 Grand Prix cars) and was killed on lap 1 when it overturned. The other Delages were withdrawn, but in any case Costantini in the nimbler 2.3-litre Bugatti was unassailable; he clipped 12 minutes off his 1925 winning time and won by over 10 minutes from two more Bugattis.

A TWELVE-CYLINDER SUNBEAM

It was Costantini (2.3 Bugatti) again in the 420-mile Spanish race at San Sebastian. Three 1925 Delages ran, while a formidable newcomer was the twin-supercharged 4-litre V12 Sunbeam, confected from two 2-litre Grand Prix type cylinder blocks set at 60 degrees on a common crankcase, and used for record-breaking, racing, sprints and hillclimbs. Segrave led the race in this versatile beast for five laps, when a wheel bearing broke up. Benoist's Delage then took over until its blower defected, when a 'wait and see' Costantini moved ahead, never to be caught.

The 'Costantini-Bugatti show' excelled yet again at Monza in the 248½-mile Milan Grand Prix, where Segrave again shone initially with the big twelve-cylinder Sunbeam, but retired half-way with an oil-less gearbox. Costantini then went on to win his last race, after which he became Bugatti's racing manager.

What amounted virtually to another *Formule Libre* race, although the organizers framed some remarkably free-and-easy 'sports car' rulings, was the first German Grand Prix. This took place at Avus, Berlin, attracting a large but curious entry ranging from small German 1100s such as Bob, Aga, Alfi and Pluto, to two NAG 'Monzas', two works-prepared, 'privately' entered 2-litre straight-eight supercharged Grand Prix Mercedes decked out with 'sporting' bodywork but no wings, a new 1½-litre Grand Prix OM from Italy, and two privately-owned 1925 Talbot voiturettes. Starters totalled an impressive forty, comparing strikingly with the three which contested the French Grand Prix a fortnight earlier.

During practice G. Platé's Chiribiri collided with an NAG, his mechanic being killed (the Germans adhered to the outdated riding mechanics rule), while in the race the combination of Avus asphalt and heavy rain brought disaster at one-third distance. With the narrow track as slippery as soap, Rosenberger's 2-litre Mercedes skidded at full speed, demolished a timekeepers' hut

Rain on the asphalt surface at Avus wrought havoc in Germany's first Grand Prix, with cars plunging right and left off the circuit. The most serious accident involved the works-backed 2-litre straight-eight Mercedes driven by Adolf Rosenberger, which slid helplessly off a turn, striking a timing hut and killing its three occupants. It brought racing at Avus to an end for five years.

85

and killed its three occupants. Chassagne (Talbot) skidded and overturned, his mechanic being injured, Mederer (Pluto) slid helplessly into a parked petrol lorry, and Urban-Emmrich (Talbot) skated right over the return road across the nose of Caracciola's Mercedes, hit a post and bounced into a packed enclosure, injuring three spectators.

Watched by Dr Porsche, Ing. Sailer and Alfred Neubauer, the future Mercedes team manager, young Rudi Caracciola won the race in true professional style, thoroughly earning his nickname *regenmeister* or 'master of the rain'. Riecken (NAG), Cleer (Alfa Romeo) and Clause (Bignan) were next home, while a quartet of blown NSUs placed 1-2-3-4 in the 1½-litre class. Nando Minoia in the Grand Prix OM made fastest lap at 100.16 mph — the first over 100 mph lap in a Continental race — but had to retire. Seventeen cars finished in all, but the accidents caused much controversy in Germany and Avus saw no more car racing until 1931.

Two end-of-season 1500 cc races which provided good exercise for the late-developing Grand Prix Talbots were the 200 Miles Race at Brooklands, when the cars were 'British' and painted green, and the 250-mile Grand Prix du Salon at Montlhéry, where they reverted to French and were painted blue! Without serious opposition they finished first and second in the '200', *l'Anglais* Segrave leading *le Francais* Divo, while Moriceau stuck the third Talbot in a sandbank, spent an energetic half-hour

Mass celebration: workers at the NSU factory at Neckarsulm join in the reception accorded the racing team following their 1-2-3-4 win in the 1100–1500 cc class of the 1926 German Grand Prix. The successful drivers were Klöble, who averaged 78.17 mph, Scholl, Islinger and Müller.

The Regenmeister (above):
Rudolf Caracciola's drive to
victory in the first German
Grand Prix at Avus under wet
and difficult conditions earned
him the sobriquet 'the
Rainmaster'. His car was one of
the 2-litre straight-eight Grand
Prix Mercedes designed by Dr
Porsche and built in 1924.

Left: Otto Merz and his
eight-cylinder Grand Prix
Mercedes, poised for the starting
signal in timed runs at the 1926
Solitude race meeting. He went
on to win the racing car event by
15 minutes from Kimpel's
Bugatti and an NSU.

Gone to earth (above): Frenchman Jules Moriceau, former Talbot-Darracq mechanic, digging his straight-eight 1½-litre Talbot out of one of the sandbanks marking the 200 Miles Race circuit at Brooklands in 1926. It cost him almost half an hour, and dropped him from third to seventh place in the results.

Opposite: Britain's most successful racing driver of the 1920s decade, H. O. D. Segrave, accepts the André Cup, premier award in the JCC 200 Miles Race, from T. B. André after winning the 1926 race in a Talbot. It was his third '200' victory.

digging it out, and finished seventh. At Montlhéry the position was reversed, Frenchman Divo leading Segrave home, with Moriceau completing the 1-2-3.

Whatever the quality of the racing, it was a good season for French cars. For the new 1100 cc voiturette class Amilcar produced a team of beautiful little racing cars, with watch-like supercharged twin ohc six-cylinder roller-bearing engines, allegedly bearing very close resemblance to one bank of the 1923–25 V12 Delage unit with bore and stroke variations. These failed first time out at Miramas, but won every other 1926 race they contested, at Boulogne, Brooklands 200, Monza and Montlhéry.

'OLD NO 7' CRASHES

In the sports car class, too, France had things all her own way. Le Mans was *'une véritable triomphe'* for the 3½-litre Lorraine-Dietrichs, which took the first three places. They were aided involuntarily by the unfortunate S. C. H. Davis, whose efforts to

Hors de combat: C. M. Harvey, winner of the 1923 200 Miles race, was less fortunate in the 1926 event. His straight-eight front-drive 1½-litre Grand Prix Alvis was baulked on its 23rd lap by a slow 7 hp Fiat at one of the artificial turns. The Alvis spun wide and struck a telegraph pole and iron railings near the timekeepers' box in the finishing straight.

retrieve second place in a brakeless 3-litre works Bentley (the famous 'Old No 7') ended disastrously with the car stuck firmly in a sandbank with 23½ hours completed and half an hour to go. Given a lift back to the pits, he reported the accident to W. O. Bentley, after which, as he so poignantly wrote later, 'I went for a long walk alone, and wished I was dead'. Poor Sammy had to wait twelve months before vindicating himself.

Two 2-litre OMs from Italy were fourth and fifth, the Bentley being placed sixth on distance. The Rudge-Whitworth Cup, based on a comparative capacity-performance formula, was awarded to the over-all winning Lorraine, but the OM company protested that Foresti/Minoia had won it. The AC de l'Ouest jury rejected their protest, so OM took the matter to the CSI. Five months elapsed before that august body finally granted them the victory, indicating that official dilatoriness is not a modern disease. The ugly little 1100 cc 'Tank' Chenard-Walckers performed outstandingly, winning the San Sebastian 12 Hours in Spain from a team of 6-litre Mercedes, OMs and other larger-engined cars. They also notched up a 1-2-3 in the Boillot Cup at Boulogne, while for the house of Peugeot André Boillot achieved a notable 'double' in 24-hour races, taking both the Belgian event at Spa and the second Italian 'Night Grand Prix' at Monza.

1927—TOUJOURS BENOIST

The second year of the 1½-litre Grand Prix Formula was certainly better than 1926, though qualified by the dominating Benoist/Delage combination and paucity of opposition. After nearly incinerating their drivers in 1926, the Delages underwent major revision by designer Lory. The cylinder heads were turned 'back to front' as it were, transferring the exhaust side to the left, while the twin Roots blowers on the left were replaced by a larger single unit mounted high at the front of the engine. Then the entire engine/transmission line was moved 4 inches over to the left to give the driver more cockpit room, and finally a handsome new inclined radiator covering the dumbirons was fitted.

With 170 bhp at 8,000 rpm available, the 1927 Delage was tremendously fast, reliable, and comfortable; it was, indeed, unassailable, and Robert Benoist enjoyed the finest racing season any driver of the 1920s could hope for — five starts and five wins. His first, in a very wet Grand Prix de l'Ouverture at Montlhéry in March, served as a 'warm up' for the four European rounds of the third World Championship. These were the French, Spanish, Italian (and European) and British Grands Prix, and in all these Benoist's ascendancy was challenged but once.

Big fours and sixes: two works four-cylinder 3.8-litre sleeve-valve Peugeots and a single 5.4-litre triple-carburettor six-cylinder Excelsior (No. 1) at the start of the 1926 Belgian 24 Hours race at Spa. Peugeot No. 2, getting away smartly, won the race in the hands of Frenchmen André Boillot and Rigal, with the Belgians Dils and Caerels second in the Excelsior.

Driver/manufacturers were scarcer in the 1920s than in modern times. Apart from his Land Speed Record-breaking Fiat of 1924, Ernest Eldridge, a talented London engineer, built two smaller 'specials' in 1925 which were raced in France, Spain and Italy, and at Indianapolis, USA. The first Eldridge Special (above) had a 1½-litre supercharged four-cylinder Anzani side valve engine, installed in a modified Amilcar 'Grand Sport' chassis. It scored a fourth place behind the Talbot trio at Montlhéry in 1925 and broke numerous class records there, but retired from the 1926 Indianapolis '500' with a broken steering knuckle.

In the French Grand Prix he led a Delage 1-2-3 from lap 4 to the finish. So obvious was their supremacy in practice that Ettore Bugatti withdrew his three cars just before the start, arousing the crowd to a storm of protest, booing, hissing and mocking whistles. *'Il a peur'* ('He's scared') went up the cry, and so, indeed, Bugatti was — scared of defeat for his cars before some 100,000 spectators. That made the race a straight Delage-Talbot fight, and all was not well with Talbot in 1927. Divo made a gesture by leading the first three laps, but thereafter Benoist with his satirical smile was in full command. One Talbot only survived, driven to fourth place by Moriceau and a talented young Englishman named Grover who called himself 'Williams' and lived in La Baule, France.

That proved to be the last appearance of the Talbots as works cars, for financial straits in the parent STD group forced their withdrawal from racing. Nothing, it seemed, could now disturb a Delage walk-over, but in the Spanish Grand Prix Benoist met vigorous and unexpected resistance from the daring Italian, Emilio Materassi, in a Bugatti. Nose to tail they duelled in the season's most exciting Grand Prix, until Materassi, with nine laps to go, overdid it and slammed into a wall. Benoist, seeing only a thick cloud of dust ahead, spun under violent braking, lost

all sense of direction, and resumed racing — the wrong way! Quickly appraised by frantic marshals, he turned hastily and went on to win from Conelli's Bugatti and another Delage.

In contrast the Italian Grand Prix at Monza was dull. Delage sent just Benoist to face an OM team and an unexpected American challenge from that year's Indianapolis 500 Miles winner, George Souders in a Duesenberg, and two Miller-based front-drive Cooper Specials. Heavy rain, poor acceleration and minimal brakes blunted the American effort, but Pete Kreis managed third place with one of the Coopers behind the Delage and an OM. Suffice it to record that Benoist won the long, wet race by no less than 22 minutes.

Then came the British Grand Prix at Brooklands, and the customary non-starters that spoiled so many races in the 1920s. The Indianapolis Duesenberg, the Talbots, two front-drive Alvises and three highly exciting twelve-cylinder Fiats were all absent from the grid. Thus it was Delage v. Bugatti again, although all the talents of Materassi and a promising young man from Monaco, Louis Chiron, could not hold the Delage trio on the wide open spaces of Brooklands. Materassi led lap 1 in a depressing English drizzle, but mercilessly the Delages passed him one after the other. New man Divo, transferred from Talbot,

The second Eldridge Special (above) looked lower and sleeker than the first, but was a disappointing car. Its 1½-litre Anzani engine had a twin ohc head which theoretically raised output by over 30 bhp to 112. Eldridge designed a special chassis giving notably low build, with dry sump lubrication and the oil tank alongside the driver, but the car retired at Monza, San Sebastian and Montlhéry in 1925. At the wheel here is Douglas Hawkes, who drove at Indianapolis in 1926 but was forced out with a seized camshaft after covering 91 of the 160 laps. Curiously, neither of the Eldridge Specials raced in Britain.

While at Indianapolis for the 1926 500 Miles race, Ernest Eldridge tried out a 2-litre straight-eight single-seater Miller. Its performance left him disenchanted with his own Anzani-engined 'Specials', and he acquired the Miller, bringing it to Europe and taking many records with it. Unfortunately he crashed in the car during a records foray at Montlhéry in 1927, losing the use of one eye and never racing seriously again.

and Bourlier both took turns at leading, but finally Benoist moved ahead and led the Delage victory formation home. Materassi's corner work was brilliant but eventually his hard-worked Bugatti wilted and broke, Chiron taking fourth place ahead of two more 'Bugs'. George Eyston and Prince Ghica (Bugattis) retired, as did Purdy and Scott with two Thomas Specials.

These low-built straight-eight 'flat-irons' bristled with ingenuity, but sadly missed the master care of their creator, J. G. Parry Thomas. That great Welsh driver and engineer had met his death earlier in 1927 when trying to regain the World Land Speed Record from Malcolm Campbell's 'Bluebird' on Pendine sands. The figure he had to beat was 174.88 mph, and it was on the second of two exploratory runs at around 170 mph that his car, the 27-litre Liberty aero-engined 'Babs', suddenly slewed, rolled over, then righted itself again, with poor Thomas mortally injured.

It was generally thought that the offside driving chain had broken and struck his head. The car was buried in the sands, and lay undisturbed for forty-two years, after which it was exhumed and restored. Evidence of the wreckage suggested that it was not the chain that killed Thomas, but rather that he suffered fatal injuries as the car turned over. Whatever the cause, a clever, kind and lovable man, and one whose memory the Welsh still revere, had been lost.

A RACE STOPPED

Three weeks after that tragedy, motor racing sustained a shock of a different kind. Listed early in the 1927 calendar on 26 March was the Grand Prix de Provence at Miramas. Had it taken place it would probably have raised Benoist's victory score to six, but as it was he was the unwitting cause of some alarming happenings. Four preliminary heats were to sort out an entry ranging from 1.1 to 3 litres, with the Final to decide the outright winners. Some separate races in the morning coincided with heavy rain, and were cancelled, but in the afternoon, although it still poured, the eliminating heats for the Grand Prix were run off, respective winners being Duray (Amilcar), Moriceau (Talbot), Lehoux (2.0 Bugatti) and Chiron (2.3 Bugatti).

Seventeen cars qualified for the Final, and while Benoist went off for a late warming-up lap in the single 1500 cc entered by Delage, the other cars were marshalled to the grid. When Benoist rounded the final corner before the starting straight he found cars drawn up right across the track; he braked desperately but the car turned broadside, hit Duray's Amilcar, and put both cars *hors de combat*. At this the three Talbots were precipitately withdrawn, presumably on grounds that the track was too dangerous. The rest were then flagged away, Chiron and Lehoux darting ahead in clouds of spray.

One up on his colleagues, the cameraman perched precariously on the post gets the best start shot of the 1927 French Grand Prix at Montlhéry. Albert Divo leads spiritedly in one of the three eight-cylinder Talbots, dogged remorselessly by the Delages of Benoist, Bourlier and Morel. As trouble hit the Talbots one by one, the Delage trio moved up to score a triumphant 1-2-3 finish.

The absence of the star Grand Prix entries incensed the unruly Marseillaise crowd, who stormed the barriers, invaded the circuit, and stopped the race. Then they attacked the Talbot pits and vented their rage by damaging other cars which had hastily pulled up to avoid running them over. Aggrieved entrants vented *their* wrath on the Miramas organizers for failing to control the crowd, and vowed never to race there again. Nor did they, the unlucky southern track remaining unused for ten years.

On the *Formule Libre* front, the mercurial Emilio Materassi shone brightly. He won the Targa Florio, his pace such that of twenty-two starters only nine finished; he won the Tripoli Grand Prix in North Africa, the Perugia Cup, Bologna circuit and

Montenero Cup races in Italy, and the San Sebastian Free-for-all Grand Prix in Spain. Fortune spurned him, however, in the Rome Grand Prix when his car, an Itala, went out of control and into the crowd, killing two; the race went to the very up-and-coming Tazio Nuvolari with a Bugatti.

A galling glimpse of 'what might have been' came with the last Free Formula race of 1927, the 50 km Milan Grand Prix run as a supporter to the Italian Grand Prix at Monza. It marked the brief but brilliant return of Fiat to racing, with a superbly modern 1500 cc twin-crankshaft, triple ohc twelve-cylinder racing car, the Tipo 806 — lower even than the Delage or Talbot, and higher in power with 187 to 170 bhp. Its driver was the great Pietro

Trier: the 1927 Indianapolis 500 Miles race winner, George Souders, brought his 1½-litre centrifugally-supercharged eight-cylinder Duesenberg to Monza, Italy, for that year's Grand Prix of Europe. Unable to hold the flying Benoist and his Delage, Souders lay second for 12 laps despite pouring rain. Then the Delage lapped him, showering the Duesenberg with spray and spume, drowning its magneto and forcing the American's retirement.

97

Four Bugattis taking the top chicane in the Brooklands finishing straight during the British Grand Prix, last big race of the 1927 season. Materassi heads the quartet, followed by Count Conelli, George Eyston and Louis Chiron. Only one Bugatti, that of Chiron, completed the 325-mile race, finishing fourth, six laps behind the all-conquering Delage trio.

Bordino, who in pouring rain simply blasted away from opposition which included a P2 Alfa Romeo, several 2- and 2.3-litre Bugattis and a Miller-engined Cooper Special; he won at 94.57 mph to Benoist's 90.04 mph in the *Gran Premio* (a much longer race) and it was perhaps significant that Benoist, although also entered for the Milan Grand Prix, had elected not to run.

That way Delage evaded possible defeat, and Fiat wound up their magnificent racing career with a final win. Three of the new

The world of motor racing was saddened when, on 3 March 1927, J. G. Parry Thomas was killed at Pendine sands in South Wales while attempting to beat the World Land Speed Record with his Liberty V12 aero-engined car 'Babs'. The popular Welshman was not only a magnificent driver at Brooklands and elsewhere but also a superb engineer, as was evident from his Leyland-Thomas and Thomas Special racing cars.

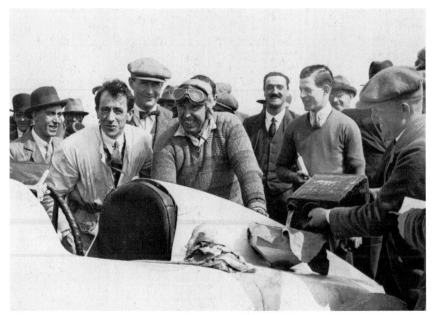

Fiat '12s' were entered for the British Grand Prix — an intoxicating prospect, although of course they non-started. Only one car was ever actually built, and legend, unconfirmed, has it that Fiat chief Agnelli, returning from a long American tour, was furious at the work put into the racing car at a time when the economic depression was already being felt, and ordered it to be broken up, together with all spares and patterns. Certainly no car or parts ever survived.

Unique in Grand Prix racing was the compulsory use of exhaust silencers in the British events at Brooklands in 1926 and 1927. Here Albert Divo, transferred from Talbot to Delage after the French Grand Prix, negotiates one of the unsatisfactory sandbank 'corners', followed by the amateur Bugatti driver Prince Ghica and Bourlier (Delage).

A grimy Otto Merz and a 6.8-litre Mercedes-Benz Type S minus at least one mudguard, after winning the second German Grand Prix, held on the new and sensational Nürburgring circuit in the Eifel district, 17.58 miles per lap and containing some 170 corners. Merz was former chauffeur to the Archduke Ferdinand, being with him at the Sarajevo assassination in 1914, while he also had a reputation as the 'strong man' of motor racing.

Above: the Miramas circuit, already blighted by the 'three-car' French Grand Prix of 1926, suffered another fiasco early the following year when the crowd ran amok and stopped the principal race. Preliminary heats for the Grand Prix de Provence were run off in pouring rain, Morel (depicted here) winning the 1100 cc event with one of the works six-cylinder twin ohc Amilcars.

'Down in the forest . . .' (right): sheer drops were no exaggeration on the famous Madonie circuit used for the Targa Florio. In 1927, after hitting a boulder which burst a tyre, French driver 'Sabipa' plunged some 50 feet from the road down into this garden with his 1½-litre Bugatti.

Above: Robert Benoist, goggles down on his face, does a warming-up lap for the Grand Prix de Provence at Miramas with the Delage. On returning to the starting area he collided with Duray's Amilcar, both cars being too damaged to race. With two Talbots also withdrawing, the indignant crowd stormed on to the circuit as the remaining field got under way, stopping the race and venting their rage on the Talbot pits.

Left: Italy's champion driver of 1927 was undoubtedly the daring Emilio Materassi of Florence, seen at San Sebastian where his challenge of Benoist's Delage made the Spanish Grand Prix one of the season's most memorable races.

THE NÜRBURGRING

Of great importance to Germany, and to motor racing as a whole, was the opening of the Nürburgring, which completely eclipsed any other road circuit anywhere. Set in the heart of the hilly Eifel region of West Germany, it began as the idea of that region's District Controller, Dr Creutz, for easing the crippling unemployment in the area, for encouraging tourism, and for providing the German motor and motorcycle industries with really adequate testing facilities. Cologne's *Oberburgermeister,* Konrad Adenauer, later to become Chancellor of Western Germany, took up the idea eagerly, and approached the German Government for financial backing.

Somehow 15 million marks were found in those hard times, and the prodigious 18-mile course, winding, twisting and plunging dementedly through virgin forest land, was built around an ancient twelfth-century castle, the ruined *Schloss* Nürburg; hence the Nürburgring. The full 17.58-mile lap, including the North and South circuits, contained 172 corners, 88 of them left-hand and 84 right-hand, and the Ring and all its facilities (paddock, pits, stands, and even a hotel), was completed in good time for the *Eroffnungsrennen,* the great inaugural weekend, on 18–19 June 1927.

Above: an aerial view of the start-and-finish area of the remarkable Nürburgring, built between 1925 and 1927 to alleviate unemployment and provide a test circuit for German industry. The long building alongside the straight is the future Sport-Hotel, with stands for thousands of spectators.

Opposite: Fiat of Turin ended an honourable career in Grand Prix type motor racing at Monza in 1927, when Pietro Bordino won a short and easy victory in the Formule Libre Milan Grand Prix. His car, an all-new 1½-litre Fiat with twelve-cylinders, twin crankshafts and triple ohc, is No. 15, lined up for the preliminary 1500 cc heat, with Bordino at the wheel talking to Felice Nazzaro. Behind are Serboli's Chiribiri and Cirio's Bugatti.

The programme was a mixture of sports and racing car events, and almost inevitably Caracciola figured among the victors, as did Werner and Momberger, and this meeting served as a useful dress rehearsal for the second German Grand Prix in July. This was International, but the twenty-one entries were chiefly German, and included seven of the new Porsche-designed Mercedes-Benz 6.8-litre supercharged 'S' models. A works 4-litre Peugeot entered for André Boillot was discreetly withdrawn, and nearly 100,000 spectators saw three bellowing white Mercedes dominate the 317-mile *Grosser Preis* in the order Merz, Werner and Walb, with Caracciola, unusually, among the retirements.

BRILLIANT LADY DRIVERS

A remarkable fourth, and winner of the 1½ to 3-litre class, was a little Czech lady named Elizabetta Junek, driving a 2.3-litre Bugatti with enviable skill. Even Teutonic efficiency was caught out by her success; the band had no music for the Czech National Anthem, but they saved the situation by playing an excerpt from Smetana's 'The Bartered Bride'! Knowledgeable spectators were less surprised, for Mme Junek had already distinguished herself in that year's Targa Florio, scarcely a woman's race, yet one in

Above: Mme Junek winning at the Montlhéry circuit in the 2.3-litre Type 35 Bugatti. Driving a similar car this Czech lady won her class in the 1927 German Grand Prix and nearly defeated all the men in the 1928 Targa Florio.

Left: the best-known woman driver of the 1920s, Mme Elizabetta Junek of Prague, Czechoslovakia, seen with the victor's bouquets after winning the Coupe des Dames *race at Montlhéry in 1927. She drove her Bugatti without overalls—note oil spots on her stockings and skirt.*

which she lay a remarkable fourth on lap 1 until her Bugatti's steering box broke. With the same car she won the *Coupe des Dames* race at Montlhéry in August, besides performing prominently at Czech hillclimb meetings.

Another lady driver, Mme Violette Morriss, achieved something equally outstanding by winning that notoriously exhausting 24 hours race in which one person only may drive one car, the Bol d'Or at Fontainebleau. Her car was an 1100 cc supercharged BNC, and she won, the only woman in the event, on sheer merit, covering 1006.27 miles in the 24 hours, and heading two other BNCs.

Clearly 1927 sports car racing was following no *status quo* in Benoist/Delage style. For Italy it meant the first Mille Miglia, that dramatic revival of town-to-town racing, which had been banned by the French after the calamitous 1903 Paris-Madrid race. This new event covered 1,000 miles of ordinary public roads, starting at Brescia and returning via a huge figure-of-eight taking in Bologna, Florence, Rome and Padua, with over 30,000 Fascist militia patrolling the course. A colossal entry of seventy-seven cars in nine capacity classes was received, and Brilli-Peri, 1925 Italian Grand Prix winner, was favourite with a 3-litre RLSS Alfa Romeo. He led to Rome, only to drop out with transmission trouble, thus early starting the Mille Miglia legend that 'he who leads in Rome never wins'. Marinoni in another Alfa also retired, and three 2-litre six-cylinder side-valve 'Superba'

France had her talented women drivers too. This is Mme Violette Morriss in an 1100 cc supercharged BNC, winning the long and gruelling 1927 Bol d'Or—the race in which one driver only is permitted throughout the 24 hours.

The Bentley Boys, 1927 (above):
a uniquely British gathering at
Le Mans before the dramatic
Bentley victory with one
surviving car. They are, left to
right, front row: F. C. Clement,
L. G. Callingham, Baron
d'Erlanger, G. Duller, S. C. H.
Davis and Dr J. D. Benjafield.
Behind d'Erlanger is Woolf
Barnato, while between Duller
and Davis is W. O. Bentley
himself.

Before calamity (left): a peep
with the spectators at Le Mans,
1927, and George Duller in
Bentley No. 2 before the
notorious White House Corner
crash at dusk. All three Bentleys
were involved, Callingham's and
Duller's being eliminated, but S.
C. H. (Sammy) Davis retrieved
his battered 3-litre and
jury-repaired it at the pits, after
which he and Dr Benjafield
drove on to historic victory.

With his face bloated by intense toothache, Andre Boillot finds it hard to smile after winning the 248-mile Sporting Commission Cup fuel consumption race at Montlhéry in 1927. His car was a four-cylinder, 2.5-litre sleeve-valve engined Peugeot with offset transmission and single-seater bodywork.

OMs scored a magnificent 1-2-3 victory, with class wins falling to Peugeot, Fiat, Bugatti, OM, Lancia and Isotta-Fraschini, the latter a huge, ill-braked 8-litre machine which reached 100 mph on roads thickly lined on each side by spectators.

For Britain it meant another Le Mans victory at last for Bentleys, beaten in 1925 and 1926 by Lorraine-Dietrich, and seemingly doomed to fail again in 1927. Three of the handsome vee-radiatored cars (a new 4½-litre and two 3-litres) took part, and all three were involved in the famous twilight crash involving six cars at White House Corner. Two were rendered *hors de combat*, but S. C. H. Davis with the last Bentley to join the mêlée extracted his battered car and limped back to the pits. Damage included a bent front axle and frame, smashed mudguard and running board, and a broken headlight, but after jury-repairs he rejoined the race, he and Dr J. D. Benjafield working up to second place.

The Chassagne/Laly 3-litre Ariès seemed to have the race secure when the Bentley was speeded up, and the French car broke down 1½ hours before the finish. Thus did Davis, Benjafield and 'Old No.7' win the race they lost in 1926, and the saga of the British green Bentleys at Le Mans was vastly enriched. The unlucky Ariès gained some compensation in class wins at Spa, Lille and San Sebastian, and two outright wins in the Boillot and Florio Cup races.

Bentleys, too, won another 24 hours race to complement their Le Mans success when that versatile jockey/driver/humorist George Duller and F. C. Clement gained the 4½-litre car its first victory in the Paris 24 Hours Grand Prix at Montlhéry. Public attendance there was sparse, and the organizers conveniently went broke just after the race, so that no prize money was ever received! Duller scored another win at Brooklands in the Essex

'Upon his heels a frightful fiend . . .'? (above): C. M. Harvey's front-drive Alvis fumes fiercely as it shapes up to pass P. L. Densham's faired-in Brescia Bugatti, coming through the sandbanks during the 1927 200 Miles Race at Brooklands.

Skegness is so bracing (left): Raymond Mays, a busy man in 1928 developing and racing the Vauxhall-Villiers, took a break at Skegness to drive Amherst Villier's 2-litre Type 35 Bugatti in the sand races there, winning the main event. His passenger is Peter Berthon, who was to be closely linked with Mays' future racing activities.

Above: Epitomizing the Teutonic sports car of the 1920s in brute power, size and noise, the supercharged six-cylinder Mercedes-Benz in the right hands was a superb performer. Here the hands of Rudi Caracciola guide an S-type to yet another 'fastest sports car' award at the 1927 Klausen hillclimb in Switzerland.

Right: this tiny British two-seater, the Jappic, weighed under 5 cwt, thanks to an armoured wood chassis and minimal alloy bodywork. With an optional 350 or 500 cc JAP single-cylinder motorcycle engine fitted, it broke 16 class records at Brooklands in 1925–26 at speeds up to 70.46 mph, driven by its designer, H. M. Walters, seen on the car, and Kaye Don.

MC's Six Hours race for sports cars, this time beating two Bentleys with a 3-litre six-cylinder twin ohc Sunbeam — the last works success achieved by that famous marque, now entering the twilight of its career.

That race also marked the last appearance in a racing car of the great H. O. D. Segrave, whose run in the second works Sunbeam ended doubtfully when he allegedly ran out of fuel on the far side of the track, and obtained some from an outside source, thereby incurring disqualification. His interests having already turned from car races to record-breaking and motor boat racing, he swiftly left the track, an action smacking of Niki Lauda's precipitate withdrawal from racing at the Canadian Grand Prix of 1979.

*   *   *

Dead car park: two Bentleys, a Frazer Nash and two French cars line the verges, while Laly's beetle-backed 3-litre Ariès comes past to win the 1927 Boillot Cup race at Boulogne. This success, coupled with others in the Florio Cup at St Brieuc and at Spa, compensated the French marque in part for its disappointment at Le Mans, where it comfortably led the Bentley with under an hour to the finish, but then broke down.

5
SPORTS CARS ASCENDANT
1928-29

Fritz von Opel driving the Opel 'Rak 2' rocket-propelled car at Avus track, Berlin, in May 1928. With its 24 powder rockets electrically fired, the car accelerated from 0 to 100 kph in 8 secs., and reached a speed of 121.2 mph. It was the second of three experimental cars developed by Opel in collaboration with rocket expert Max Valier and pyrotechnics engineer Frederich Sander.

Increasing gloom on the business front and a general tightening of purse strings took the 'Grand' right out of Grand Prix racing during the remaining years of the 'Roaring Twenties'. For 1928 ACF tried to run its annual classic at Comminges to AIACR rules, stipulating racing cars free of capacity restriction but with a weight limit of between 550 and 600 kg, and a distance of at least 375 miles. This could have produced a fair race, but only six entries came in. Instead, then, they substituted a tiresome sports car formula, involving individual handicaps, four eliminating heats and a 163½-mile Final, with no pit stops allowed for fuel or repairs, and all tools to be carried on the car.

When Opel ended rocket car research and joined General Motors their test driver Kurt C. Volkhart, a former racing driver and engineer, built his own rocket car on Valier principles. He used an old German-built Bugatti Type 22 chassis called a Rabag, retaining the engine and transmission for over-all mobility, and gave demonstrations at fairs and carnivals around Germany in 1929, his exploits including taking a lady passenger for an 80 mph rocket run along part of the Nürburgring.

Amazingly, twenty-eight starters materialized, although just one was a factory entry — the supercharged Bugatti of that French-domiciled Englishman 'W. Williams', frequently called 'the Anglo-French enigma'. He won from the scratch mark by over 2½ minutes from a Salmson, Stutz, Lombard and two Chryslers, which indicates what a mixed field it was.

The only 1928 race actually run to the AIACR's 'Formule Libre with strings' was September's Italian/European Grand Prix Monza, which attracted twenty-two starters and 120,000 spectators. This, again, could have been a good race, but for a terrible accident involving Emilio Materassi and his ex-works eight-cylinder 1½-litre Grand Prix Talbot. While passing Foresti's Bugatti at around 120 mph the Talbot apparently touched wheels, shot off course, jumped a protective ditch and dashed into the crowd. Twenty-three died, including Materassi himself, and over twenty were injured.

On the way up: Italian motorcycle racing ace Tazio Nuvolari gained his first 'place' in a classic car race when he finished third with this red-painted Type 35 Bugatti in the 1928 Grand Prix of Europe at Monza. Ahead of him were two famous contemporaries, Louis Chiron and Achille Varzi.

The other two Talbots, which had been purchased from STD for a stable headed by Materassi, were withdrawn, and Chiron (Bugatti) and Varzi (P2 Alfa Romeo) duelled for the lead, the Frenchman eventually winning, while third came Nuvolari (Bugatti) — three future aces showing early form. Bugatti thus won the 'World Championship' again (the last time the official contest was run) while Louis Chiron was proclaimed Champion of Europe, with further wins at Rome, Garoupe, Marne and San Sebastian to justify the choice.

It was a bad year for Italy, who lost another ace driver in Pietro Bordino before the Alessandria race in April. With Fiat's withdrawal from racing he had switched to a Bugatti, and during practice he collided with a large Alsatian dog, which jammed his steering. The Bugatti plunged over a parapet into the River Tanaro, the unfortunate Bordino being pitched out and drowned. Thereafter the Alessandria race, which was held up to 1934, became known as the Coppa Bordino.

Plain racing car events without irksome weight limits still thrived in Italy and France, the warring Bugattis, Alfas and Talbots all getting a share of success. The newer Bugattis took the lion's share, but Campari's basically 1924 P2 Alfa won at Pescara, while the Talbots performed better in private Italian hands than when raced by STD from Suresnes. Before his death in the Monza calamity, Materassi had won both the Mugello and Montenero races with an engine enlarged to 1750 cc, as well as taking the 1½-litre classes at Rome and Alessandria, while motorcyclist Arcangeli added firsts at Cremona and a class win at Pescara.

It would have been interesting to see how the Talbots and Delages compared in private hands, but unfortunately no such confrontation occurred. Malcolm Campbell had acquired one of the 1927 Grand Prix Delages which had been sold off at the close of the season, and he scored two wins in the Boulogne Grand Prix and the Brooklands 200 Miles race. These proved just too easy for him, with no worthwhile opposition, and domination by a topline Grand Prix possibly contributed to the demise of both these events after that year. Boulogne had run short of money, enthusiasm and entries, while the circuit was woefully out of date. As for Brooklands, the '200' was drawing far fewer entries, with little encouragement for amateurs, while spectator attendance, too, had markedly diminished.

Boulogne's last Speed Week: this typically informal motor racing fixture of the 1920s ran from 1920 to 1928. The very mixed entry for the National Trophy race at the final meeting included Bugattis, Salmsons, Amilcars, a Bucciali, a La Licorne, sundry French cyclecars—and Malcolm Campbell's ex-works 1½-litre Grand Prix Delage, which won the 334½-mile race by 6½ minutes from a 2-litre unsupercharged Bugatti and the rest.

At the St Martin hairpin: Malcolm Campbell in the process of winning the Boulogne National Trophy race in the Delage. Despite losing 3 minutes stopped on the circuit tracing a loose ignition wire, he never had to extend the car fully, although his fastest lap at 78.18 mph was never equalled on the old 23¼-mile Boulogne circuit.

Mme Junek from Prague once again enhanced the new-found respect for women racing drivers by her achievement with a 2.3 Bugatti in her second Targa Florio. Like Stirling Moss and Denis Jenkinson in the 1955 Mille Miglia, she prepared detailed notes on the course kilometre by kilometre during practice. On lap 1 of the race she lay fourth, but on lap 2 she was *leading*. On lap 3 Campari (Alfa Romeo) caught her, but she stayed second until on the fifth and final lap the Alfa burst a tyre. Alas, good fortune deserted Mme Junek too, her car suffering a defective water pump. Precious minutes passed while she found water and topped up, while Frenchman Albert Divo, standing in for the late Pietro Bordino, came up hand over fist and won. Three more cars passed, and after her epic drive the Czech lady had to rest content with fifth.

Just a week later two French *Bugattistes* gave the 'men only' racing adherents another shock in the Burgundy 4 Hours race run on an eleven-mile circuit outside Dijon. Despite the presence of the illustrious Chiron, whose Bugatti gave trouble, Mme Janine Jennky won the race outright, while Mme Lucy Schell, mother of the well-known post-war racing driver Harry Schell,

won the 1500 cc class. Britain had her distinguished 'Atalantas' too; Miss May Cunliffe, the Hon. Mrs Victor Bruce and Mrs W. B. Scott all won races at Brooklands, and did much more besides. May Cunliffe was a prominent performer on Southport sands and elsewhere with Bentley and Sunbeam cars; Mrs Bruce was a successful endurance driver on road and track, she and her husband, the Hon. Victor Bruce, breaking seventeen long-distance world records with an AC from 4000 to 15,000 miles at Montlhéry, in an icy ten-day spell at Montlhéry in December 1927. Mrs W. B. (Jill) Scott was brilliant on Brooklands, setting a ladies' record there at 120.88 mph in 1928, driving her husband's 2-litre Grand Prix Sunbeam; she was the first woman driver to gain the 120 mph badge, and won several races with Amilcar, Bugatti and the Sunbeam.

A SWING TO SPORTS CARS

The mounting economic gloom caused a notable swing from racing to sports car events. Racing cars had to be specially built, and were costly to buy, to maintain and to transport. Sports cars were cheaper, being developed from production models, and could

Graduate from the 1100 cc class, and a future Grand Prix star, burly Luigi Fagioli from Gubbio passing through Campofelice during the 1928 Targa Florio in a 1500 cc Type 26B Maserati. He finished seventh over-all and fourth behind three Bugattis in the 1½-litre class.

117

'Grandmother' was the nickname given to this Mercedes 'sprint special' raced by Adolf Rosenberger between 1927 and 1930. It had a 1914 4½-litre four-cylinder Grand Prix Mercedes engine with supercharger added, in a 1924 Targa Florio-type four-wheel braked chassis, and is seen competing in the 1928 Klausen hillclimb in Switzerland.

be driven to and from the circuits. In many eyes, also, they benefited design more usefully than supercharged multi-cylinder racers, and provided a 'lesson as well as a spectacle' in one scribe's words.

Le Mans was, of course, the 'champion' of such events, and the 1928 race profited greatly from the participation of American Stutz and Chrysler cars in opposition to the 4½-litre Bentleys, with Lagonda, Alvis and Aston Martin also joining in. Woolf Barnato and B. Rubin were lucky to win in one Bentley with its frame cracked and radiator badly leaking, hard pushed to the end by the 4.9-litre Stutz of Brisson/Bloch, while two 4.1-litre Chryslers were next home. There was some stimulating technical variety, the first three cars having respectively four, eight and six cylinders, the class-winning Alvis and Tracta both had front-wheel drive, and the 1100 cc class-winning BNC was super-charged.

The lady vanquishes (above): a scene from the 1928 4 Hours Grand Prix of Burgundy, run on an undulating 11-mile circuit near Dijon. The leading Bugatti is driven by Mme Janine Jennky, and in pursuit is Louis Chiron, dashing Monégasque and European champion elect that season. Madame kept her head and her lead, while Chiron had trouble and dropped back.

Left: Mme Jennky with her 2-litre Type 35 Bugatti before the race. She averaged 76.5 mph for the 312 miles of the Burgundy 4 Hours.

Le Mans 1928 proved a great struggle between the 4½-litre four-cylinder Bentleys and the American 4.9-litre straight-eight Stutz and 4-litre six-cylinder Chrysler cars. Above is the Bentley of Woolf Barnato and Bernard Rubin, which finally clinched the marque's third 24 Hours victory despite a cracked chassis and an empty radiator. The Stutz was second and two Chryslers third and fourth.

A significant absentee was the 1½-litre six-cylinder twin ohc supercharged Alfa Romeo entered by the romantically named Boris Ivanowski, an expatriate Russian with great driving talent and the resources to indulge it. The lovely little Alfa 'six', designed by Jano, had already won the second Mille Miglia, the Modena race (driven by Enzo Ferrari), the Circuit of Sicily, and the Essex Six Hours race at Brooklands (Ramponi driving). The Le Mans scrutineers, however, saw fit to reject Ivanowski's car at the last moment on some petty seating irregularity, so he took the rejected Alfa on to Spa for the Belgian 24 Hours race, with Marinoni as co-driver.

Nothing could hold them; they defeated twenty-nine other cars with engines of up to 4.1 litres, and won by 145 miles from two Chryslers. Ivanowski went on to win the final Boillot Cup race at Boulogne and the 'Bad Roads Race' at Lille, helping to establish the 1500 cc Alfa as unofficial 'sports car of the year'. It had not yet penetrated into Germany, land of the big white Mercedes, however, which faced instead a challenge from four works Bugattis. It might be expected that seasoned drivers like Brilli-Peri, Chiron, Conelli and Minoia in supercharged 'Bugs' which were virtually Grand Prix models with wings fitted could hold off the great lumbering 2-ton 7-litre 'Mercs' on the tortuous Nürburgring, but the German defence was surprisingly strong.

Above: Brisson's menacing black Stutz cornering at Pontlieue during the Le Mans 24 Hours of 1928. Co-driven by Bloch, this American newcomer to the Sarthe circuit fought a lone fight against three seasoned Bentleys. It held the lead through much of the night, and finally finished second despite losing all but top gear in its 3-speed gearbox.

Left: one of Britain's most successful Brooklands women drivers in the late 1920s, Mrs W. B. (Jill) Scott, in the 2-litre Grand Prix Sunbeam with which she set a new Ladies' Outer Circuit record at 120.88 mph in 1928, when winning the Essex MC's 10 lap handicap. She also scored wins with 2-litre Bugatti, six-cylinder 1100 cc Amilcar and 1½-litre GP Delage cars, and broke several class records.

In a merciless 5-hour race run in a heat wave, Mercedes-Benz won the first three places. The co-victors, Caracciola and Werner, both had to stop for medical attention, one with heat exhaustion, the other with a wrenched shoulder sustained while hauling his massive steed through the endless corners. The Bugattis, troubled by overheating brakes, only managed fourth, sixth and seventh places, while Tim Birkin, the first Englishman to race on the Nürburgring, was eighth with his 4½-litre Bentley and first unsupercharged finisher. His riding mechanic, incidently, was Wally Hassan, later of Jaguar and Coventry Climax fame. A tragic accident cost the life of the Czech driver Cenek Junek, who had just taken over the Bugatti from his wife Elizabetta, but lacked her skill. As a result of his death Mme Junek gave up motor racing, depriving the sport of a brilliant woman *pilote*.

THE TT REVIVAL

The race that really lifted 1928 racing from mediocrity was the revived Tourist Trophy. If Britain lost her Grand Prix, with few regrets other than from spectators, she gained a road racing classic that vastly enriched her racing history in the next decade. With antiquated English law forbidding racing on public roads, the RAC went not to the Isle of Man, as in the past, but to Northern Ireland, where a magnificent road course was mapped out in the Ards district of Belfast. Measuring 13.7 miles per lap, it was to be covered 30 times, giving a distance of 410 miles.

Change of mount (below) for S. C. H. Davis. The 1927 Le Mans co-winner with a Bentley chose a front-drive 1½-litre unsupercharged Alvis for 1928, sharing the race with W. Urquhart Dykes. They finished ninth over-all and second in the 1500 cc class behind their Alvis team-mates Harvey and Purdy. 'The front drive would take corners beautifully steadily provided that the engine was pulling', Davis later wrote about this pioneer British exponent of front wheel drive, so widely used today.

Above: classic road racing returned to the British Isles in 1928, when the RAC Tourist Trophy was revived as a 410-mile sports car race on the splendid 13.7-mile Ards circuit outside Belfast. Forty-four cars took part, and among the numerous '1100s' were nine low-chassis 'Brooklands' Riley 9s. W. P. Noble in one makes a pit stop.

Left: 'The Anglo-French Enigma' they called 'W. Williams', the successful Bugatti driver who won two French Grands Prix and the first Monaco Grand Prix. He spoke perfect French and lived at La Baule, but was an Englishman whose real name was William Grover; he is seen in 1928 on a picturesque part of the Cap d'Antibes circuit overlooking the Mediterranean.

The reaction was remarkable. Instead of perhaps ten Grand Prix cars and the inevitable non-starters, fifty-six entries were received, representing every British sporting marque, plus Mercedes-Benz, Stutz, Austro-Daimler, Bugatti, FN, Amilcar, Tracta and OM from abroad. An estimated 250,000 people attended the race, including 10,000 from across the water, in glorious weather. Forty-four starters in five classes, co-drivers in the passenger seats, made an endless, fascinating stream of cars. Hoods had to be erected for the first two laps, then folded away; crashes were legion, for this was real road racing and British drivers brought up largely on Brooklands had little experience of high speed cornering, and spirited in-fighting developed in every class.

On a cliff-hanging final lap, Kaye Don's 1½-litre supercharged Lea-Francis fled over the line, victor by just 17 seconds from Leon Cushman's 1½-litre supercharged front-drive Alvis, which stopped, completely dry of petrol, 300 yards past the flag. An Austro-Daimler trio placed 3-4-10, securing the team prize, and Birkin's Bentley was fifth, while class winners were Riley, Lea-Francis, OM, Austro-Daimler and Bentley. Writing of the first Ulster TT in *The Autocar,* S. C. H. Davis justly called it 'the race of the year'.

1929 — GRAND PRIX MORATORIUM

Grand Prix racing, as the AIACR wanted it, reached its nadir in 1929. Seemingly imbued with the virtues of economy in that bleak period of the twenties, they devised one of their dreaded fuel consumption formulae. Cars were allowed 14 kg of petrol and oil per 100 km, the petrol to be of commercial type with a density of 720 @ 15°C; they had to weigh at least 900 kg empty, two-seater bodies 100 cm wide were required, and tails would not be worn. Instead a special exposed bolster fuel tank redolent of

Nadir: degeneration of the French Grand Prix, once the season's great classic, climaxed in 1929 when the ACF devised a fuel consumption formula requiring the use of exposed bolster-type fuel tanks with huge petrol gauges displayed. Thus equipped, André Boillot's old 4-litre Peugeot looked even older; it finished second in the race, held at Le Mans, behind 'Williams' (Bugatti).

TT winners and losers: Kaye Don, the outright winner of the 1928 Ulster TT in his 1½-litre supercharged Lea-Francis, leads Louis Dutilleux's Type 43 2.3-litre Bugatti at Dundonald. Don won a race lasting almost 6 hours by a mere 13 secs. from L. Cushman's front-drive Alvis, with two Austro-Daimlers driven by Hugh Mason and Cyril Paul third and fourth.

The TT being for so-called 'touring' cars, hoods had to be erected for the first two laps. Three entrants therefore decided to save time by running saloons, these being a Riley Monaco, a Belgian FN and (hottest of them all in perhaps two senses) this closed Frazer Nash driven by T. H. Aldington and Eric Burt. It retired with a collapsed piston.

When Malcolm Campbell stopped to lower his hood after the first two laps his Type 43 suddenly burst into flames. A split in the fuel tank (almost full) caused petrol to leak onto the hot exhaust pipe, the blaze being so fierce that the fire crew could not control it, and the car was totally destroyed. Surprisingly, considering that its owner had business interests in car sales and insurance, and was a Lloyds underwriter, the Bugatti was uninsured.

All sorts and sizes: the start of the 1929 Burgundy Grand Prix shows Guy Bouriat in a Grand Prix Bugatti (No. 40) shooting up to pass two Le Mans-type Chryslers and a big Mercedes-Benz four-seater. Behind another pack of sports cars are several more racing Bugattis, including one driven by the son of financier Baron Henri de Rothschild, running under the nom de course of 'Philippe'. He won at 86 mph, even impressing his father, who was opposed to his racing activities.

On the Futa pass: the 2-litre Maserati driven by Baconin Borzacchini and Ernesto Maserati leading the 1929 Mille Miglia—Italy's unique 1000-mile road race. They were first at Bologna, Florence and Rome, then had to retire at Terni, thereby giving early credence to the legend that 'he who leads at Rome never wins the Mille Miglia'. Campari and Ramponi eventually won with an Alfa Romeo.

the heroic pioneer days of racing had to be carried at the rear, bearing a monster petrol gauge! The sole freedom was in engine capacity.

Small wonder that the Italians rejected these rules and ran their races their way, or that the Germans and British carried on sports car racing. Only two events, the French and Spanish Grands Prix, complied with this weird Formula, and both proved farcical. The once-exalted Grand Prix de l'ACF took place on the Le Mans circuit over 375 miles, and at 5000 francs entry fee they were lucky to attract sixteen entries and eleven starters. 'Williams' and his Bugatti won a dismal race at 82.66 mph, with his fastest lap at 86.93 mph. (Murphy's 1921 winning average of 78.11 mph and lap record of 83.40 mph on the same circuit were achieved in far rougher conditions.)

La Course dans la Cité: 1929 brought a unique new race to the calendar, the Monaco Grand Prix, through the streets of Monte Carlo. On the left is the winner, 'Williams', in his Bugatti, painted green in confirmation of his English nationality. The floppy cap worn back to front was an essential part of his racing equipment.

Stripped 'sports': the Italian Goffredo Zehender drove this 1750 cc six-cylinder Alfa Romeo at Monaco, with wings, lights and other road equipment removed. Unable to match the pace of the Bugattis, he retired out on the circuit with transmission trouble.

Boillot's old 4-litre Peugeot was second, disturbing an all-Bugatti finish of six cars only. In Spain thirteen Bugattis, an Alfa Romeo and a Delage set off in pelting rain to win the King's Cup and 10,000 pesetas. Eight finished, all Bugattis, with Louis Chiron the victor followed by one 'Philippe', who was, in fact, the son of Baron Henry de Rothschild the Paris financier. 'Philippe' was a driver of considerable talent, but his father disapproved of his racing, hence the pseudonym. On learning that he intended to compete in the Burgundy 4 Hours race at Dijon in May that year, the Baron had sent a minion to stop him. He arrived too late, for 'Philippe' had already won the race by a length from Bouriat and Gauthier, the parental wrath being somewhat appeased on learning this!

Free Formula races, uninhibited by footling restrictions, continued to flourish. Indeed, a fantastic new race was born, one which still exists and stands unique in the motor racing calendar. This was the Monaco Grand Prix, an audacious project of M. Antony Noghès, founder-president of the AC Monaco. Anxious to bring racing (and thus tourists) to the tiny principality of Monte Carlo on the French Mediterranean coast, he schemed out a tortuous 2-mile circuit through the Monaco city streets, announcing his race for 14 April 1929. *La Course dans la Cité* was received in some quarters with scorn, scepticism, or a shaking of heads; 'such presumption, such folly. Half the cars would be put out on the first lap, and the rest on the second . . .'

The streets were barricaded with sandbags and hoardings, bridges were built across the streets for access to the all-important Casino, and the tramways were stopped. Sixteen starters, all supercharged, comprised eight Bugattis, four Alfa

Sensation of the first Monaco Grand Prix was undoubtedly Rudolf Caracciola and his Mercedes-Benz. He wielded the massive 7.1-litre SSK as though it was a light car, snatching the lead from 'Williams' for five laps, but dropping back to finish third after a lengthy pit stop to refuel and change rear tyres.

Romeos, and one each of Delage, Maserati, La Licorne and Mercedes-Benz. The latter, a stripped SSK 7.1-litre sports car, seemed wildly unsuitable for so serpentine a course, save that its driver was Rudi Caracciola. Only one Bugatti was an actual works entry, that of 'W. Williams', who confirmed his nationality by having his car painted British green.

'Williams' and Caracciola 'made' the race, the Englishman taking the lead with the German thrilling the crowd by his efforts to catch the lighter Bugatti, the banshee wail of the Mercedes supercharger echoing off the buildings. On Lap 30 'Caratsch' got past to lead for five laps before 'Williams' retook him, and all chances of a Mercedes win then dissolved in an abnormally long pit stop. An excellent race, with but two minor crashes to confound the 'jonahs', ended in the order 'Williams', Bouriano (Bugatti) and Caracciola, with 'Philippe' fourth and four other finishers.

Victor and runner-up: two top-line Italian racing drivers after the exhausting 243-mile Rome Grand Prix of 1929. On the left, winner Achille Varzi takes a good long satisfying draught of vino—*or is it* aqua minerale? *On the right, Count Gastone Brilli-Peri, second home 47 secs. behind, simply looks tired. Both drove P2 Grand Prix Alfa Romeos of 1924 origin, Brilli-Peri's having its engine slightly bored out, thereby winning the special over-2-litre class.*

An American at home: the Indianapolis 500 Miles became more and more specialized in the late 1920s, and European efforts with road racing cars more hopeless. The 1929 race was the last run to 91 cu.in. (1½-litre) rules. This Duesenberg with which Fred Winnai finished fifth typifies the American breed. It had offset transmission and a complex intercooler arrangement for the supercharger.

An American abroad: George Stewart, alias Leon Duray, alias 'the Black Devil', brought two front-drive Millers to Europe for the Monza Grand Prix in 1929. The cars were fast but brittle, and he had to retire after a spectacular display. The picture, taken during tests at Montlhéry, shows the Miller front drive layout, with reversed de Dion-type axle sprung by quarter-elliptics, and the inboard brakes.

BRILLI-PERI v. VARZI

Italian racing was as spirited as ever, something of a personal duel developing between Count Brilli-Peri, who raced both a P2 Alfa Romeo and one of the ex-Materassi Talbots, and the young Achille Varzi, who had sold his racing motorcycles to buy a P2. 'Brilli' won at Tunis, Tripoli and Mugello with the Talbot, and at Cremona with his P2, but Varzi retorted with 'firsts' at Alessandria, Rome and Montenero. The 'decider' was the Monza Grand Prix, a race organized in defiance of the AIACR in place of the Grand Prix of Europe, and split into three capacity heats with a Final for the nine fastest cars.

Brilli-Peri and Varzi, both in P2s, were at it hammer and tongs from flagfall, but 'Brilli' had a tyre burst when leading and Varzi tore past. His rival then lost more time with a broken exhaust pipe, and Varzi won his first big race, with Nuvolari (Talbot) second, Momberger's vast Mercedes third and the unlucky Brilli-Peri fourth. Extra interest was provided by the extrovert American Leon Duray, whose real name was George Stewart and who called himself 'the Black Devil' and wore all-black overalls and helmet. He brought two purple-painted single-seater front-drive Miller-based Packard Cable Specials to Europe, one a '1500', the other a 2-litre. Accompanying him to look after them was Jean Marcenac, the Frenchman who had gone to the USA in 1920 to fit front brakes to de Palma's Ballot for the Elgin road race, and had decided to settle there.

Duray broke the Monza lap record on his third practice round, and led his heat in the smaller-engined car, only for it to break down. He then drove the other car in the 2-litre heat, climbing to third place, although he could not catch the older P2s fighting it out ahead. Duray dropped to fourth and finally retired, but his efforts were not entirely in vain. Coveting the straight-eight twin-cam Miller engines, and knowing that Duray needed cash, Ettore Bugatti offered the American sufficient for his needs, plus three 2.3-litre Type 43 sports Bugattis in exchange for the two Packard Cable Specials. Duray accepted, selling the 'Bugs' in California, while Bugatti copied the Miller twin ohc heads for his Type 50 and 51 cars of 1930–31, and kept the cars at Molsheim for years. Nearly thirty years later the author Griff Borgeson rescued the two cars, grimed with age but still complete, and brought them back to the USA for restoration, both being treasured museum pieces today.

Another stirring performer at Monza was a new Maserati, its massive bonnet covering a formidable 4-litre four-cam 16-cylinder twin-supercharged engine. Strictly there were two

Power pack (above): two Maserati 2-litre straight-eight supercharged engines, their crankshafts geared together, made a formidable 4-litre sixteen-cylinder free formula racing car, the Sedici Cilindri.

Line-up for the unlimited heat of the Monza Grand Prix, featuring the sixteen-cylinder Maserati and three Mercedes, No. 54 being the 1914-based 'Grandmother'.

power units, two of Maserati's 2-litre straight-eights, coupled side by side with their crankshafts geared together. The result was the *Sedici Cilindri*, a splendid 'blood and sand' Formule Libre racer with which Alfieri Maserati just left his rivals standing in his Monza heat, only to lose speed suddenly on the final round, being 'pipped' on the line by Momberger's Mercedes. In the Final Maserati led the entire pack until forced to the pits with trouble, but the car behaved better at Cremona three weeks later, when driver Borzacchini broke the world's 10 km record during the race at 152.09 mph.

THE GLORY THAT WAS ENGLAND

The sports car racing world (even the French had given up calling them 'touring' cars) had its excitements too, although Le Mans was almost a walkover for an impressive phalanx of British green Bentleys. Three eight-cylinder Stutz, now with twin ohc, 32-valve heads, provided the only opposition, but two retired and the third took a trouble-dogged fifth place. Ahead were four great rumbling Bentleys, Barnato and Rubin in the newest, biggest 6½-litre Speed Six winning, with three 4½-litre cars completing a 1-2-3-4 victory formation. This was 'the Glory that was England' epitomized, with the big but superbly proportioned cars totally dominating the classic *Vingt-Quatre Heures*. Ettore Bugatti, that artist-in-metal, dismissed the Bentleys as 'Europe's fastest lorries', but they were bred and built that way to win Le Mans year after year, and to travel fast and dependably on the world's roads, and the large number surviving today testifies to their remarkable stamina.

Yanks on the Sarthe: Le Mans in the late 1920s was much enlivened by the entry of American cars, such as these two 4-litre Chryslers seen in the 1929 race. They were prepared in France, being fitted with lighter wings and quick-release wire wheels. No. 12, driven by de Vere/Mongin, finished seventh, while the other car placed sixth in the hands of Le Mans expert Henri Stoffel and Grand Prix champion Robert Benoist.

Le Mans start (above) – but the scene is Phoenix Park, Dublin, in July 1929, with the 1½-litre section of the first Irish Grand Prix for sports cars getting under way. Nearest camera are four neat-looking supercharged 'Hyper' Lea-Francis, with beyond them three Alfa Romeos, one of which won the race driven by Ivanowski.

Great moment (left): the race is run and won, Bentleys have taken the first four places, British green has triumphed again. Woolf Barnato and Tim Birkin with the winners' bouquets look understandably pleased after Le Mans, 1929.

The starting flag has dropped, and 67 drivers and riding mechanics dash across the road to 67 cars – the remarkable scene which opened the second Ulster TT in 1929. Hoods, already erected, had to be furled before the cars got away. The white cars in the foreground are the Arrol-Asters of E. R. Hall and Norman Garrad; behind are two Model A Fords, then five Bugattis. Rain made the course very treacherous, and the winner was regenmeister *Rudi Caracciola (Mercedes-Benz) from Campari (Alfa Romeo) and two Austin Sevens.*

Le Mans apart, interest focused on Great Britain, where sports car racing did not merely thrive but positively boomed. To the brilliant Ulster TT was added not one but *two* more major races — yet all three attracted first-rate entries. Having terminated their 200 Miles Race series, the enterprising Junior Car Club sought to bring 24-hour racing to England. Foiled by that maddening law forbidding racing on public roads, they hit on using Brooklands track and splitting the race into two 12-hour halves, thereby avoiding breach of by-laws which protected precious local residents by forbidding racing there at night.

As a substitute 'Le Mans' it could only be a compromise, lacking the atmosphere and glamour of real road racing through day and night, but the JCC were rewarded by over fifty entries and an excellent race. Class handicaps were imposed, so that the fastest cars were not necessarily leading — a situation easy for Brooklends *habitués* to grasp, but baffling for the many lay spectators. Bentley and Alfa Romeo sparred for places during the first 12 hours, the Italian Giulio Ramponi gaining a narrow lead, with a Bentley and another 1500 cc Alfa deadheating for second when the cars were shepherded to the paddock for an overnight stay under guard.

The second half developed into a close struggle between the S. C. H. Davis/R. Gunter 4½-litre unblown Bentley and Ramponi in the blown Alfa '1500', the result being in doubt right to the finish.

Driving the entire race unrelieved, with his unhappy co-driver Count G. Lurani tensely unemployed ('Giulio was not even tired, but I was exhausted!', said Lurani later) Ramponi won by .003 on the handicap formula, or 3½ miles in the 24 hours, the Bentley averaging 81.39 mph to the Alfa's 76.0 mph.

Above: British road racing at its finest. The tightly-packed field storms through Mill Corner on lap 1 of the 1929 Ulster TT, the leaders heading uphill towards Bradshaw's Brae – and already one car, Bezzant's Aston Martin, has gone off on the outside of the bend. The crowd, estimated to exceed 500,000, lined the course thickly throughout its 13.3-mile lap length.

Left: two 1½-litre six-cylinder supercharged Alfa Romeos lead the Saorstat Cup race which constituted the 1500 cc heat of the 1929 Irish Grand Prix at Phoenix Park. Giulio Ramponi leads Boris Ivanowski at Gough Corner, but the Italian later spun on the melting tar road, and the Russian won. The statue has been thoughtfully protected by sandbags.

Whatever prompted the Royal Irish Automobile Club to promote the Irish Grand Prix — perhaps it was the brilliant success of the Ulster TT — it proved an excellent venture. The Phoenix Park course in Dublin itself was fast, wide and safe, while spectators could be controlled and persuaded to pay admission fees. There were two separate races for up to and over 1500 cc, and British Bentleys, Lagondas, Lea-Francis, Aston Martins, Rileys and Austins confronted some formidable Alfa Romeos, with private Austro-Daimler, Bugatti, OM and Mercedes entries adding to International interest. Like the Double 12, the handicap produced a close fight between Alfa Romeo and Bentley, with hot sunshine and melting tar adding to the excitement and sending many a car spinning. The nimbler Alfa Romeos triumphed, Ivanowski the Russian scoring a notable 'double'. He took the 1½-litre race from two Lea-Francis, while in the Grand Prix he fled before a ravening Bentley quartet, winning by 14 seconds from a determined Glen Kidston in the Speed Six.

Despite the sudden plethora of British sports car races (the Brooklands 6 Hours was also squeezed in somehow, bringing a Bentley victory), the Ulster TT in August was even better than in 1928. Sixty-five starters comprised nine British and nine foreign makes, including official Mercedes-Benz, Alfa Romeo and Bugatti entries. Continental driver superiority was emphasized

The Germans gave their 1929 Grosser Preis at Nürburgring the bonus title of the Grand Prix of the Nations. Despite strong defence by Mercedes, the Bugatti team dominated the 316½-mile race, Chiron winning from 'Philippe', with Momberger's Mercedes disrupting a French 1-2-3 victory parade by beating Bouriat's Bugatti home. The over-3-litre start scene here features four massive 'Mercs' and an optimistic Estonian entry of a 9.1-litre Renault '45' tourer driven by Eduard Klimberg, which lasted one lap only.

by the results, *regenmeister* Caracciola winning in the wet with 7 litres of Mercedes, the burly Italian Campari being second in a 1750 cc Alfa Romeo. Two little supercharged Austin Sevens travelling like scalded cats placed third and fourth, followed by three more Alfas.

In treacherous wet-and-dry conditions there were incidents galore; Bentley-men Kidston and Rubin had phenomenal escapes when their massive charges ran out of road. 'I've never seen a telegraph pole get out of the way quicker' quipped Kidston, but future record-man John Cobb was less lucky, his Riley hitting one side-on. Strong man Otto Merz from Germany, who had chauffeured Archduke Ferdinand of Austria when he was assassinated at Sarajevo in 1914, battered a front mudguard on his Mercedes against an iron water pump. He tore it off with his bare hands and slung it in the back, later having to tie it back in place. A Stutz caught fire, and an OM hit a kerb and capsized, four men striving to right it unfortunately being injured when another car skidded into it from behind, two lives being lost. Despite drivers of the calibre of Divo, 'Williams' and Conelli the three works Bugattis were flagged off. Asked his opinion of the Ards circuit, Caracciola said 'Beautiful'. Campari, motoring from London to Liverpool in his Alfa, was late for the boat; police clocked him at 106 mph through a 20 mph stretch but could not catch him. . . .

A US rarity: among the American cars entered for Le Mans 1929 was this massive white Du Pont, with 5.3-litre Continental side valve straight-eight engine. Drivers were Charles Moran and Alfredo Miranda, New York distributor for the marque. Aluminium coachwork was by the Merrimac Body Co., and the boat-tail housed a 45-gallon fuel tank, here being filled before the race. The Du Pont was running eighth in the fourth hour, but ballast shifted, broke through the floor and cracked a transmission casing.

British '500': start of the 3- to 5-litre class in the first British Racing Drivers' Club 500 Miles race on the Brooklands outer circuit. Bentley No. 31, driven by F. C. Clement and J. Barclay, was the winner at 107.32 mph. The white cars 28 and 29 are Sunbeams, and No. 32 is Tim Birkin's supercharged 4½-litre Bentley, with two more Bentleys behind.

SPA MISFORTUNES

The latent perils of the hilly, winding Spa circuit in Belgium were emphasized in the 1929 Belgian 24 Hours race, when the same wet-and-dry conditions as at Ulster prevailed throughout the night run. Of four sleeve-valve Minervas entered, one skidded, killing a gendarme, continued, skidded again and somersaulted four times; one bogged down in a field; one ended deep in a ditch; the fourth, still running at the finish, was disqualified for being helped out of another ditch by several spectators. Former Delage Grand Prix driver Robert Benoist demonstrated his versatility by winning the race in an Alfa Romeo shared by Marinoni.

Grand Prix experience paid off in another important 1929 race — the fourth German Grand Prix, grandiosely sub-titled the 'Grand Prix of the Nations', for obscure reasons. After their humiliating defeat by Mercedes-Benz in 1928 the Bugatti team returned to the Nürburgring with three blown 2-litre cars, Chiron, Bouriat and that very professional amateur, 'Philippe', in the cockpits. Two Maseratis and two Alfa Romeos came from Italy in private hands, and once again defence of the Fatherland was in Mercedes-Benz' hands.

Only Caracciola could stave off the Bugatti menace this time; he led for four laps, while Louis Chiron deftly and delicately threaded his neat way through the field into second place. Then a most uncharacteristic broken connecting rod put 'Caratsch' out of the race, and Chiron moved ahead. 'Philippe' closed up behind, and only the dogged August Momberger in his Mercedes prevented Bouriat from making it a 1-2-3 victory for the *auslanders*.

One other 1929 race of vastly different character (but again it was in Britain) demands mention. In the same month that the Wall Street crash in New York spread alarm and despondency world-wide, the young and exclusive British Racing Drivers' Club (BRDC) ran their first 500 Miles Race on the Brooklands Outer Circuit — a glorious, uninhibited, very punishing full-throttle affair with no corners, braking or gearchanging to worry about. There were five handicap classes, and Brooklands being rough, bumpy, very fast and hard on cars, big heavy ones such as Bentleys and the V12 4-litre Sunbeams were favoured.

Twenty-eight spruce starters became nine jaded finishers, with three others flagged off, their 500 miles still uncompleted. Springs, axles, frames and tyres, let alone engines and the drivers and riding mechanics (optional), suffered a fiendish racking, and in a survival of the fittest Frank Clement and Jack Barclay in a

Big 'boots': the two 4-litre twelve-cylinder Sunbeams wore wide-section tyres for the 1929 500 Miles race. Cyril Paul, back to camera, finished third in the nearest car, sharing with John Cobb; the other Sunbeam, driven by Kaye Don and Dudley Froy, was forced out after 68 laps when a rear spring broke on Brooklands' merciless bumps.

Right: Lesser men than Bergmeister Stuck found hazards abounding on the long Continental climbs. The driver of this special six-cylinder Steyr with swing rear axles did a comprehensive job of wrapping a barrier around it during the 1929 Gaisberg meeting in Austria. He was unhurt, save in pride.

4½-litre Bentley won at 107.32 mph, making Britain's '500' easily the world's fastest race; and that despite a horrifying 120 mph spin on the banking by Barclay, during which he ducked down into the cockpit in expectation of overturning. A 6½-litre Bentley driven by Sammy Davis and Clive Dunfee was second, also making fastest lap at 126.09 mph, and third came Cyril Paul and John Cobb, 'tiptoeing' gingerly home in a 4-litre twelve-cylinder Sunbeam with a cracked chassis. Broken springs on two cars, two fires, a broken crankshaft, broken radiator, burnt-out pistons and broken valves were among the reasons for retirement, but despite the mechanical carnage that '500' emerged as a British neo-classic and a very satisfactory winding-up of the last season of the 'Roaring Twenties'.

The victors shared £350, the second-place men won £100, and the third £50; motor racing was so *very* different half a century ago. . . .

* * *

King of the Mountains (above) or Bergmeister they called the Austrian driver Hans Stuck, who became the acknowledged master of Continental hillclimbing, scoring innumerable FTDs in German, Swiss, Czech and Austrian events with this 3-litre six-cylinder Type ADMR Austro-Daimler.

Opposite: during a somewhat lurid drive in the 1929 500 Miles race at Brooklands, Jack Barclay in the big 4½-litre Bentley got into a hair-raising 120 mph skid on the Members' banking. He ducked down into the cockpit in case the car turned over; but he regained control and went on to share victory with Frank Clement.

142

POSTSCRIPT

Out in the wide world beyond motor racing the skies had darkened. It was not war this time — that lay ten years ahead still — but a major economic recession. Investments went down the drain, countless companies including many car manufacturers slid down the slope to liquidation. 'Cut costs and economize' became the dismal watchword, luxury car markets were decimated, and motor racing in such conditions seemed wasteful extravagance.

Nevertheless, it did not die; amateurs still found money to race, and a few manufacturers still built new racing cars, albeit smaller and cheaper. The third and fourth places by two Austin Sevens in the 1929 Ulster TT had special significance; the age of the 'baby' Austin, MG Midget and Riley 9 was dawning in British racing, and handicapping acquired new importance.

The crisis took its toll; Bentley, greatest of British racing marques, lords of Le Mans, with yet another victory there — their fifth — in 1930, were allowed to die for want of a few thousand pounds. Sunbeam, that other 'wearer of the green' and proud Grand Prix winner, withered on the ailing STD tree and was sold off, together with Talbot. In the States great names like Stutz and Duesenberg perished. Other companies drew in their horns and waited for better times, but in Italy unquenchable enthusiasm and Mussolini's hyperpatriotic spur brought new Grand Prix cars, first from Maserati, then Alfa Romeo. The 'Roaring Twenties', carefree decade of a new peace, of *laissez-faire* and 'San fairy Ann', of brilliant designs and dramatic races, was over.

*　　　*　　　*

The cover of the 1928 German Grand Prix programme, a lean production printed in monochrome as befitted those austere times.

INDEX

Figures in italics refer to page numbers of illustrations.

AC cars, *40,* 55, 72, *72*
Agnelli, Giovanni, *22,* 99
ALFA cars, 3, *3, 24*
Alfa Romeo cars, 3, *14,* 36, *44,* 45, *45,* 46, *47,* 48, *49, 50, 51,* 58, 59, 60, 61, 62, *63, 64,* 76, 114, 120, *127,* 130, 131, 134, 135, *135,* 136, 137, 138
Alfonso XIII, King of Spain, 39, *55*
Alvis cars, ix, 39, *39,* 41, *55, 67,* 76, *90, 109,* 118, *122,* 124
Amilcar cars, 22, *80,* 88, 95, *100*
André, T.B., *89*
Aosta-Grand St Bernard hill-climb, *26*
Ariès cars, 108, *111*
Ascari, Alberto, *53*
Ascari, Antonio, xii, *44, 45,* 46, *47,* 48, 50, *50, 53,* 59, 60, 61, *63, 64*
Aston Martin cars, *19,* 21, *34, 35, 78,* 80
Austin cars, 7, 41, 137
Austro-Daimler cars, 25, 26, 124, *141*
Avus races, Germany, 14, 15, *15,* 27, *40,* 85, 86

'Babs' land speed record car, 94
Baccoli, M., *6*
Bad Roads Race, see *Circuit des Routes Pavées*
Balestrero, Renato, *82*
Ballot cars, *viii,* xii, xiii, *1,* 4, *4,* 5, 9, *9, 10, 18,* 20, 21, 37
Barclay, Jack, 138, 139, *140,* 141
Barnato, Woolf, *107, 120,* 132, *133*
Beacon Hill hillclimb, *7*
Belgian Grand Prix, *17,* 19, 58

Belgian 24 Hours race, 65, 90, *91,* 120, 138
Benjafield, Dr J. D., *107,* 108
Bentley, W. O., ix, *107*
Bentley cars, ix, *16, 17,* 18, *26,* 43, 44, 53, 54, 65, *68, 72,* 88, 90, *107,* 108, *111,* 118, 120, *120,* 122, 124, 132–40, *133, 138, 140*
Benz cars, *32, 34,* 36, *69,* 71, 73
Bignan cars, 12, 13, *13,* 70, 86
Birkin, H. R. S., 122, 124, *133*
BNC cars, *68,* 106, *106,* 118
Boillot, André, xiii, 22, *25,* 29, 90, *91,* 104, *108, 124,* 128
Bol d'Or 24 hours race, 22, 42, 106, *106*
Bordino, Pietro, *10, 22, 25, 29,* 31, *33, 34,* 35, 36, 57, 58, *62,* 97, 98, *102,* 114, 116
Borzacchini, Baconin, *126,* 132
Boulogne races, 13, 55, *68, 111,* 115, *115, 116,* 120
Bouriat, Guy, *126,* 128, 139
Bourlier, Edmond, *59,* 77, 94
Brescia Voiturette Grand Prix, *10,* 11, 34, 35, *37*
Brilli-Peri, Count Gastone, 59, 62, 106, 120, *129,* 130
Brisson, Edouard, 118, *121*
British Grand Prix, 17, *78,* 79, *79,* 80, 91, 93, 94, *98,* 99, *99*
British woman drivers, 117
Brooklands racing, miscellaneous, 1, 2, *2, 12, 21, 26, 27, 40,* 52, 63, *66, 69, 70,* 110, *110,* 111, 134, 136
Brooklands 200 Miles Race, 15, 28, *38,* 39, *39,* 40, 41, 52, *56,* 64, *67,* 86, *88, 89, 90, 109,* 115
Brooklands 500 Miles Race, *138,* 139, *139,* 140, 141

Bugatti cars, 6, *6, 10,* 11, *18,* 20, 26, *29,* 32, *46,* 48, *48,* 55, 63, *65, 66, 75, 76,* 76–85, *78, 81,* 92–7, *96, 98, 100, 101, 102,* 104, *105, 109,* 113, *113,* 114, *114, 115,* 116, *119,* 120, *123, 125, 126,* 127, *127,* 128, 129, 138
Bugatti, Ettore, *6,* 48, 55, 63, 92, 131, 132
Burgundy 4 Hours Grand Prix, 116, 117, *119, 126,* 128

Cagno, Alessandro, 35
Campari, Giuseppe, 3, *24,* 46, *51,* 59, 114, 116, 137
Campbell, Malcolm, 1, 2, *2, 12,* 38, 78, 80, 115, *116, 125*
Caracciola, Rudolf, 27, *43,* 53, 86, *87,* 104, *104, 110,* 128, *128,* 137, 138
Chassagne, Jean, 5, *18,* 19, 28, 29, 65, 86, 108
Chenard-Walcker cars, 12, 24, 43, 65, *68,* 90
Chiribiri, Deo, *15, 103*
Chiribiri cars, *15, 22, 26,* 85
Chiron, Louis, 93, 94, 95, *98,* 114, 116, 120, 128, 138, 139
'Chitty Chitty Bang Bang', *8*
Chrysler cars, 118, *126, 132*
Circuit des Routes Pavées, 24, *28, 58,* 120
Circuito Bajo-Panadès, Spain, *ix*
Clement, F. C., 43, 53, 54, *107,* 109, *138,* 139
CMN car, *x*
Coatalen, Louis, 11, 30, 39
Cobb, John, 137, 140
Conelli, Count Caberto, 65, *69,* 93, 120
Coppa Florio race, *25, 29*

Corsican Grand Prix, 12, 13, *13,*
Costantini, Bartolomeo, 51, *55,*
65, 75, 77, *82–5*
Culver City 250 Miles race, *53*
Cummings, Miss Ivy, *72*
Cunliffe, Miss May, *72*

David cyclecar, *ix*
Davis, S. C. H., 64, 65, 88, 90, *107,*
108, *122,* 124, 134, 140
d'Avanzo, Baronessa Maria
Antonietta, *14*
Delage, Louis, *55,* 59, 79
Delage cars, 32, *42, 45, 47,* 47,
58–62, *64, 65, 67, 74, 75, 76,*
78–84, *78,* 91–5, *96, 99, 101,*
115, *116*
de Palma, Ralph, *xi, xiii, 1,* 4, *4,* 5
de Paolo, Peter, 57, 58
de Tornaco, Baron, *17*
de Vizcaya, Pierre, *10, 18, 23,* 26,
77
Diatto cars, 62, 82
Divo, Albert, 19, *34,* 39, *45, 55,* 62,
64, 67, 78, 79, 86, 88, 92, 93, 94,
95, 99, 116
Don, Kaye, *vi,* 124, 125
du Berry, M., *13*
Duesenberg cars, *xii, 1,* 5, 7, 8, *8,* 9,
9, 34, 57, 61, *63,* 93, *97, 130*
Duff, John F., 43, 44, 53, 54, 65
Duller, George, *56,* 65, *107,* 109,
110
Du Pont car, *137*
Duray, Arthur, 95
Duray, Leon, *130,* 131

Ego car, *43*
Eldridge, E. A. D., *70, 92, 94*
Eldridge Special cars, 62, 76, *92,*
93
Elfe cyclecar, *14*
Elgin Road Race, USA, 5, *7*
Excelsior car, *91*
Eyston, G. E. T., *78,* 80, 94

Fagioli, Luigi, *117*
Fairbanks, Douglas, *xi*
Ferrari, Enzo, *x,* 3, *3, 44,* 46, 52
Fiat cars, xi, xii, *3, 10, 19, 20,* 21,
22, 29, 31, *33,* 34, *34,* 35, *37, 38,*
39, 46, 50, 58, *59, 62, 70,* 76, 93,
97, 98, 99, *102*

Florio Cup race, see Coppa Florio
Ford car, *27*
Foresti, Giulio, *18*
Fornaca, Ing. Guido, *33*
Frazer Nash, Archie, ix, *2,* 15
Frazer Nash car, *125*
French Grand Prix, 1, *1,* 7–9, *8, 9,*
16, *18, 19, 20,* 20–2, *29, 30,* 30–2,
31, 35, 45, *45, 46, 47, 49, 50, 51,*
55, 60, 61, *65,* 66, 76, *76,* 77, 91,
92, *95,* 112, 124, *124,* 127, 128
Friedrich, Ernest, 6, *29, 46, 47*

Gallop, Clive, *19*
Garda circuit race, *15*
German Grand Prix, 71, *84,* 85, *85,*
86, 87, *99,* 104, 120, 122, *136,*
138, *142*
GN cars, x, *2*
Goux, Jules, *75, 76,* 77, 79, 82, 83
Graf & Stift car, *27*
Grand Prix des Cyclecars, 12, *12,*
27
Grand Prix of Europe, *33, 34,* 58,
63, 64, 74, 75, 77, *97,* 113, 114,
114
Grand Prix of the Night, Monza,
54, 55, *60,* 90
Grand Prix de Provence,
Miramas, 95, 96, *100, 101*
Grand Prix des Voiturettes, Le
Mans, 5, 6, *6, 11,* 27, 28
Guinness, Algernon Lee, *19*
Guinness, Kenelm Lee, *11, 17,* 28,
51, 52, *54, 56, 59*
Guyot, Albert, *viii, xiii, 8,* 13, *13,*
36, 37

Halford, F. B., *78,* 80
Halford Special car, 76, *78,* 80
Harvey, C. M., 41, *67, 90*
Hassan, W., 122
Hawkes, W. D., *17, 93*
Hindenburg Cup Race, Germany,
66, 70, 71
Hispano-Suiza cars, *75*
Horner, Franz, *69*
Hotchkiss car, *73*

Imperia-Abadal car, *17,* 19
Indianapolis 500 Miles Race, *viii,*
xi, xii, 4, *4,* 33, 34, 57, 58, *62, 92,*
93, 93, 94, 130

Irish Grand Prix, *133, 135,* 136
Irving, J. S., *56, 61*
Isotta-Fraschini special car, *23,* 27
Isotta-Maybach car, *69*
Italian Cyclecar Grand Prix, *41*
Italian Grand Prix, 9, *10,* 16, *22,*
23, 24–6, 35, 36, *52,* 61, 62, 80,
81, 82, 91, 93, 113, 114
Italian Voiturette Grand Prix, *10,*
25
Ivanowski, Boris, *68,* 120, *135,* 136

Jano, Vittorio, 46
Jappic car, *110*
Jennky, Mme Janine, 116, *119*
Joerns, Carl, *57*
Joyce, J. A., *40,* 55
Junek, Mme Elizabetta, 104, *105,*
106, 116, 122

Kidston, Glen, 63, *66,* 136, 137
Klausen hillclimb, *110, 118*
Klöble, G., *40, 86*
Kop hillclimb, 73

Lancia cars, *58*
La Turbie hillclimb, *14*
Lautenschlager, Christian, *25*
Lea-Francis cars, 124, *125, 133,*
136
Le Champion, L.C.G., *69*
Le Mans 24 Hours Race, 42, 43, 65,
68, 88, 90, 108, 118, 120, *120,*
121, 122, 132, *132, 137*
Leyland-Thomas car, *70*
Lorraine-Dietrich cars, *2,* 65, 88,
90, 108

Maggi, Count Aymo, 63, *83,* 84
Marinoni, Attilio, *51,* 106, 138
Maserati, Alfieri, 23, 27, 62, 82,
132
Maserati, Ernesto, *126*
Maserati cars, 80, *81, 83, 117, 126,*
131, *131,* 132
Masetti, Count Giulio, *20, 44,* 61,
64, *67,* 84
Materassi, Emilio, 62, 82, 93, 94,
96, 96, 97, *97, 98, 101,* 104, 113,
114, 137
Mays, Raymond, *72,* 109
Mercedes cars, *25,* 31, 48, 50, *52,*
71, 73, *85, 87, 118,* 131, *131*

Mercedes-Benz cars, 73, *99,* 104, *104, 110,* 120, 122, *126,* 128, *128, 131, 136,* 137, 138
Merz, Otto, *87, 99*
Milan Grand Prix, 97, 98, *102*
Mille Miglia, 106, 108, *126*
Miller cars, 34, 36, *37, 53,* 57, 83, *94, 130,* 131
Milton, Tommy, 61, 62
Minoia, Ferdinando, *32*
Miramas circuit, 52, 76, *76,* 77, 95, 96, *100, 101*
Moir, H. Kensington, *12, 68*
Momberger, August, 71, *71,* 104, 132, 139
Monaco Grand Prix, *127,* 128, *128*
Montlhéry circuit, 52, 60, 65, *69,* 86, 88, 91, *105,* 106, *108,* 109
Mont Ventoux hillclimb, *42*
Monza Grand Prix, 130, *131*
Morel, André, 22, *55,* 78, *100*
Moriceau, Jules, 19, *78,* 86, 88, *88,* 92, 95
Morriss, Mme Violette, 24, 106, *106*
Mugello circuit race, 3, *3, 23*
Murphy, Jimmy, *1,* 9, *9,* 36, 52
Mussolini, Benito, *22*

NAG cars, 54, 55, *60,* 71, 85, 86
Nazzaro, Felice, *19, 20, 21, 23,* 26, *102*
Noble, W. P., *123*
NSU cars, *40,* 70, 71, *71, 84,* 86, *86*
Nürburgring circuit, 103, *103,* 104, *104*
Nuvolari, Tazio, 52, 97, 114, *114,* 131

O'Donnell, Eddie, *7*
OM cars, 11, 76, 80, *82,* 85, 86, 90, 93, 106, 108, 124
Opel, Fritz von, *15, 57, 112*
Opel, Heinz von, *15*
Opel cars, *15, 57, 112*
Opelbahn track, Germany, *57*

Packard car, *xi*
Parma-Poggio di Berceto hill-climb, *x,* xii
Paul, Cyril, *139,* 140
Penya Rhin Grand Prix, *35,* 39
Perkins, W. F., *17, 61*
Peugeot cars, xii, xiii, 22, 25, 29, 90, *91,* 104, *108, 124,* 128
'Philippe', 128, 129, 138, 139
Porsche, Dr Ferdinand, 48, 86

Ramponi, Giulio, *50, 53,* 134, 135, *135*
Resta, Dario, *35,* 39, 52, *59, 61*
Riecken, E., 54, 55, *60,* 86
Riley cars, *123,* 124
Rolland-Pilain cars, 32, 36, *36*
Rome Grand Prix, 84
Romeo, Ing. Nicola, 3, 45, *53*
Rosenberger, Adolf, 70, 85, *85, 104, 118*

'Sabipa', *81,* 82, 83, *100*
Salamano, Carlo, *38*
Salmson cars, 12, *12,* 15, 27, *28, 41,* 55
San Sebastian Grand Prix, 36, *36,* 37, 51, *54,* 97
Santa Monica race, xi, *xi*
Scales, J. E., *26, 59*
Schell, Mme Lucy, 116
Scott, Mrs W. B, 117, *121*
Segrave, H. O. D., *11,* 15, *20,* 29, *30,* 31, *35, 45,* 47, 51, *54, 55, 56, 59,* 64, *72, 79,* 80, *82,* 84, 85, 86, *89,* 111
Shelsley Walsh hillclimb, *72*
Sitges circuit, *34, 36, 37,* 39, 52
Solitude races, Germany, *69,* 71, *87*
Souders, George, 93, *97*
Spanish Grand Prix, *37,* 39, 62, *67,* 78, *82,* 91, 92, *96, 97, 101,* 127, 128
Stuck, Hans, *141*
Stutz cars, 118, *121,* 132

Sunbeam cars, *16, 17,* 18, *18,* 19, *20,* 21, *21,* 29, 30, *30,* 31, *31, 34,* 39, *45,* 46, 47, 51, *54, 61,* 62, *67, 72, 82,* 84, 85, 111, *121, 138, 139,* 141
Swiss Voiturette Grand Prix, 52, *59*

Talbot-Darracq and Talbot cars, 11, *11,* 15, 19, 28, 29, *35,* 39, 52, *56, 59,* 64, 65, *69,* 76, *78,* 79, *79,* 80, 85, 86, *88,* 92, 95, 96, 113, 114
Targa Florio, xii, *5, 24, 25, 44,* 48, *81,* 82, *82, 83,* 84, 96, *100,* 104, 116, *117*
Thomas, J. G. Parry, *56, 70,* 94, *98*
Thomas, René, *viii,* xii, xiii, *xiii, 4, 5, 11, 30, 42,* 78, 79
Thomas Special cars, 76, 94
Tourist Trophy races, *16, 17,* 18, 19, 122, *123, 125, 134, 135,* 136, 137

Vandervell, G. A., *27*
Varzi, Achille, 114, *129,* 130, 131
Vauxhall cars, *16,* 18
Voisin cars, *21,* 22, *30,* 32
Volkhart, Kurt, *113*

Wagner, Louis, *9, 49,* 61, 78, *78,* 79, 80
Werner, Christian, 34, 48, 71, 104, 122
Wilcox, 'Howdy', xii, *xiii*
World Championship, 57, 61, 62, 76, 78, 80, 83, 91, 114
'W. Williams', 92, 113, *123, 127,* 129

Zborowski, Count Louis, *8, 35, 37,* 39, 50, *52*
Zehender, Goffredo, *127*